NATIONAL TEAMS OF THE WORLD

NATIONAL TEAMS OF THE WORLD

Edited by
Nicola von Velsen

Texts by
Michael Brepohl

Illustrations by
Paul and Dirk Uhlenbrock

PRESTEL
Munich · London · New York

CONCACAF

Uᴇ

CONMEBOL

A

AFC

CAF

OFC

CONTENTS

AFC
Asian Football Confederation

CAF
Confederation of African Football

ALG	Algeria	122
ANG	Angola	124
BDI	Burundi	126
BEN	Benin	128
BFA	Burkina Faso	130
BOT	Botswana	132
CGO	DR Congo	134
CHA	Chad	136
CIV	Ivory Coast	138
CMR	Cameroon	140
COD	Congo	142
COM	Comoros	144
CPV	Cape Verde	146
CTA	Central African Republic	148
DJI	Djibouti	150
EGY	Egypt	152
EQG	Equatorial Guinea	154
ERI	Eritrea	156
ETH	Ethiopia	158
GAB	Gabon	160
GAM	Gambia	162
GHA	Ghana	164
GNB	Guinea-Bissau	166
GUI	Guinea	168
KEN	Kenya	170
LBR	Liberia	172
LBY	Libya	174
LES	Lesotho	176
MAD	Madagascar	178
MAR	Morocco	180
MLI	Mali	182
MOZ	Mozambique	184
MRI	Mauritius	186
MTN	Mauritania	188
MWI	Malawi	190
NAM	Namibia	192
NGA	Nigeria	194
NIG	Niger	196
RSA	South Africa	198
RWA	Rwanda	200
SEN	Senegal	202
SEY	Seychelles	204
SLE	Sierra8 Leone	206
SOM	Somalia	208
SSD	South Sudan	210
STP	São Tomé and Príncipe	212
SUD	Sudan	214
SWZ	Swaziland	216
TAN	Tanzania	218
TOG	Togo	220
TUN	Tunisia	222
UGA	Uganda	224
ZAM	Zambia	226
ZIM	Zimbabwe	228

CONCACAF
Confederation of North, Central America and Caribbean Association Football

AIA	Anguilla	232
ARU	Aruba	234
ATG	Antigua and Barbuda	236
BAH	Bahamas	238
BER	Bermuda	240
BLZ	Belize	242
BRB	Barbados	244
CAN	Canada	246
CAY	Cayman Islands	248
CRC	Costa Rica	250
CUB	Cuba	252
CUW	Curaçao	254
DMA	Dominica	256
DOM	Dominican Republic	258
GRN	Grenada	260
GUA	Guatemala	262
GUY	Guyana	264
HAI	Haiti	266
HON	Honduras	268
JAM	Jamaica	270
LCA	St. Lucia	272
MEX	Mexico	274
MSR	Montserrat	276
NCA	Nicaragua	278
PAN	Panama	280
PUR	Puerto Rico	282
SKN	St. Kitts and Nevis	284
SLV	El Salvador	286
SUR	Suriname	288
TCA	Turks and Caicos Islands	290
TRI	Trinidad and Tobago	292
USA	United States	294
VGB	British Virgin Islands	296
VIN	St. Vincent and the Grenadines	298
VIR	US Virgin Islands	300

CONMEBOL
Confederación Sudamericana de Fútbol

ARG	Argentina	304
BOL	Bolivia	306
BRA	Brazil	308
CHI	Chile	310
COL	Colombia	312
ECU	Ecuador	314
PAR	Paraguay	316
PER	Peru	318
URU	Uruguay	320
VEN	Venezuela	322

OFC
Oceania Football
Confederation

ASA	American Samoa	326
COK	Cook Islands	328
FIJ	Fiji	330
NCL	New Caledonia	332
NZL	New Zealand	334
PNG	Papua New Guinea	336
SAM	Samoa	338
SOL	Solomon Islands	340
TAH	French Polynesia / Tahiti	342
TGA	Tonga	344
VAN	Vanuatu	346

UEFA
Union of European Football
Associations

ALB	Albania	350
AND	Andorra	352
ARM	Armenia	354
AUT	Austria	356
AZE	Azerbaijan	358
BEL	Belgium	360
BIH	Bosnia and Herzegovina	362
BLR	Belarus	364
BUL	Bulgaria	366
CRO	Croatia	368
CYP	Cyprus	370
CZE	Czech Republic	372
DEN	Denmark	374
ENG	England	376
ESP	Spain	378
EST	Estonia	380
FIN	Finland	382
FRA	France	384
FRO	Faroe Islands	386
GEO	Georgia	388
GER	Germany	390
GIB	Gibraltar	392
GRE	Greece	394
HUN	Hungary	396
IRL	Ireland	398
ISL	Iceland	400
ISR	Israel	402
ITA	Italy	404
KAZ	Kazakhstan	406
KOS	Kosovo	408
LIE	Liechtenstein	410
LTU	Lithuania	412
LUX	Luxembourg	414
LVA	Latvia	416

COUNTRIES A-Z

Gabon	160	Laos	68
Gambia	162	Latvia	416
Georgia	388	Lebanon	70
Germany	390	Lesotho	176
Ghana	164	Liberia	172
Gibraltar	392	Libya	174
Greece	394	Liechtenstein	410
Grenada	260	Lithuania	412
Guam	44	Luxembourg	414
Guatemala	262		
Guinea	168	Macau	72
Guinea-Bissau	166	Macedonia	420
Guyana	264	Madagascar	178
		Malawi	190
Haiti	266	Malaysia	74
Honduras	268	Maldives	76
Hong Kong	46	Mali	182
Hungary	396	Malta	422
		Mauritania	188
Iceland	400	Mauritius	186
India	50	Mexico	274
Indonesia	48	Moldova	418
Iran	52	Mongolia	78
Iraq	54	Montenegro	424
Ireland	398	Montserrat	276
Israel	402	Morocco	180
Italy	404	Mozambique	184
Ivory Coast	138	Myanmar	80
Jamaica	270	Namibia	192
Japan	58	Nepal	82
Jordan	56	Netherlands	426
		New Caledonia	332
Kazakhstan	406	New Zealand	334
Kenya	170	Nicaragua	278
Kosovo	408	Niger	196
Kuwait	66	Nigeria	194
Kyrgyzstan	60	North Korea	92
		Northern Ireland	428
		Norway	430
		Oman	84

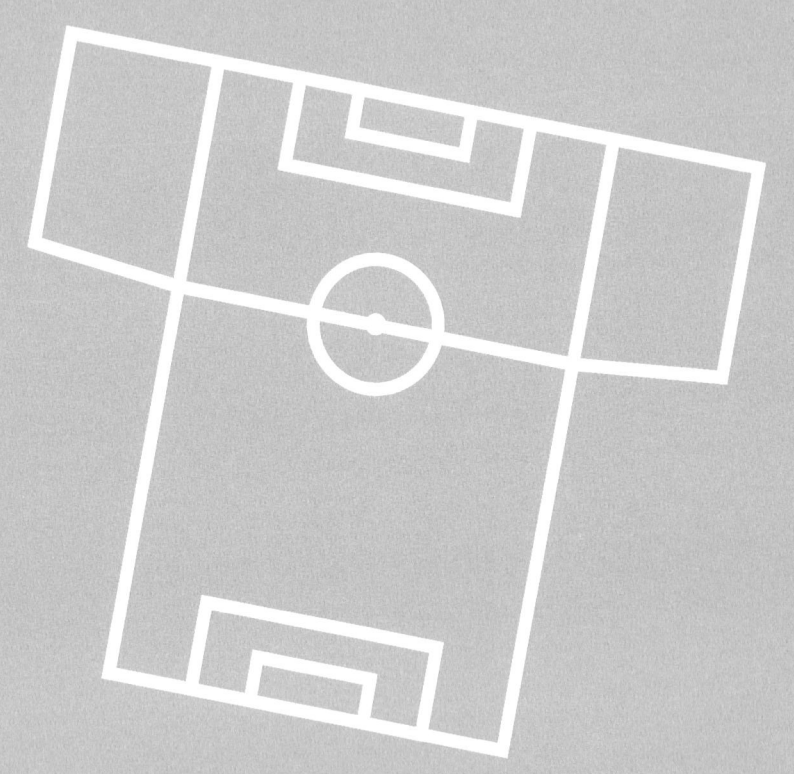

Warm Up

This is not a fashion book, but it does contain the world's most desirable fabrics. After all, anyone passionate about football has at some point dreamt of pulling on their country's national football shirt. It is many an armchair fan's dream not to watch the match from home, but to be out there banging in the goals and kissing the shirt in front of millions of adoring fans.

There are countless Nobel Peace Prize winners who will undoubtedly make a much more valuable contribution to the progress of humanity, but you can bet your bottom dollar that not a single one of them will be worshipped anywhere near as much as Pelé, Ronaldo, Sir Bobby Charlton, Maradona, Beckenbauer, Drogba and the like. They have become immortal (in their own lifetimes). Their heroics on the football field far outshine any shortcomings they may have had during or even after their playing careers. Every great star has enjoyed success at club level. The true glory they are associated with, however, will never disappear even decades after they have won the World Cup in the shirt of their national team.

This book contains the glorious shirts of 223 footballing nations. It should be noted that the football world differs in some ways from the political and even from the known geographical world. Looking at the football associations, for example, Europe is anything but a community. Not even the United Kingdom is united. It contains four rival national teams. In terms of geography, there is also the odd continental drift and shift. In Israel's case, it is a member of UEFA and has been for decades, due to the tense situation of the Middle East. There are also states in Asia that are part of the European association.

Like most players in the world, we have made ourselves subject to FIFA rules in the creation of this book, which means we are only showing shirts of those teams who are full members of the world federation. Therefore, we offer apologies to the fans of Palau, Nauru, the Vatican City and 11 other countries for not showing their teams in this book.

In arranging this book, we have followed the six federations of FIFA, which are: AFC (Asian Football Confederation), CAF (Confederation of African Football), CONCACAF (Confederation of North, Central America and Caribbean Association Football), CONMEBOL (Confederación Sudamericana de Fútbol), OFC (Oceania Football Confederation) and UEFA (Union of European Football Associations).

We have also adhered to the FIFA table (taken 1 December 2017) with the world rankings, knowing that some experts may consider rival rankings more efficient. However, what would football be without making those tough decisions that regularly get people's blood boiling? Wrong decisions are all part and parcel of football. Would we still be talking about the Wembley final of 1966, had it not been influenced by a Russian linesman awarding a goal for a ball the whole of which never crossed the line? Or the flipside when Frank Lampard netted against Germany at the World Cup in 2010 and it was disallowed even though it was a mile inside the net? In the absence of goal-line technology for books, we take this opportunity to apologise in advance, should we ourselves make any blatant mistakes in this book. Even in this age of globalisation, information about soccer matches played out even in the farthest corners of the South Seas or the remotest regions of the Himalayas can often be spurious and contradictory.

Our world is round and keeps turning as does a football. The cut-off date for our book was 1 December 2017. In the meantime, it may be that American Samoa need not worry about having the record for the highest ever defeat because another team has lost a game by a margin of more than 31 goals. In a word: if you really need to stay exactly on the ball, we recommend you check the internet for any of the latest developments. Although, in the wake of fake news, perhaps we ought to paraphrase the usual copyright disclaimer and state that not all the facts in this book were necessarily right even at the time of going to press.

Brief History of Football Dress

The creation of the football shirt involved several European nations. In many European countries, it is called a 'Tricot', coming from the French meaning to knit (tricoter). Whereas in the English speaking world a football shirt is often called a jersey, coming from the knitted wool cloth of the Channel Island of Jersey. Either way, the original knitting style involved a special combing technique of the fabric, which provided for elasticity in the material and allowed the shirts to fit tightly around the body and for easier movement when playing sport.

The first uniform type of sportswear probably originated from Germany. Friedrich Ludwig Jahn, the father of German gymnastics, clothed his fresh, pious, happy and carefree gymnasts in homogeneous, grey linen kits. But, of course, we have to credit England, the founding home of football, with inventing the football kit. At the same time as Jahn's fit young athletes paraded around the gym in attractive team outfits, cricket teams started to show up in England wearing uniforms too. The first football kits were copied directly from the cricket teams and some English sources suggest that the first football teams wore caps, which is a privilege left only to goalkeepers in the modern age and that only to block out the sun (or in Petr Cech's case, a specially designed protective headguard, after he suffered a severe skull fracture).

Charlie Roberts of Manchester United played an important role in the evolution of football dress. At the turn of the century, he was the first player to run out wearing shorts, similar to the way we see them today. In some ways, he could be seen as the male predecessor to Mary Quant, who 60 years on would be responsible for the development of the miniskirt.

Roberts' adopted hometown was nicknamed 'Cottonopolis' and cotton was indeed the most important material for decades when it came to football kits. However, when it came to tournaments held in hot countries, cotton had its drawbacks. With every storming run over the course of 90 or 120 minutes, sweat absorbed jerseys would become heavier and heavier. From the 70s onwards, shirts were made using plastics, initially highly durable polyamide and today breathable micro-fibre polyesters.

Big Business

There are clear financial motives for clubs and national teams to be changing their kits on a regular basis. Top European teams turn over tens of millions each year through the sale of their players' jerseys. And to ensure demand is stable, new looks are brought in continually. However, only a slight fraction of the huge sales from shirts actually goes back to the Third World countries where they are produced, often in appalling conditions. Some of the proceeds will be used to finance the huge transfer fees demanded nowadays for top stars. Sometimes, a not insignificant amount will then be turned over again for the shirt sales of these newly signed players. A few national football associations make handsome profits from the kits of their star players, but fans of the many African and Asian international teams simply cannot afford the prices to prove their love of football. Whilst clubs in the domestic leagues tend to have a few new kits for each season, the national side will generally present a new one before the start of a major tournament. This book shows all of the shirts to be worn at the 2018 World Cup in Russia, as provided by their national associations up until 1 December 2017.

Rules and Regulations

Players may only appear in garments authorised by the official rules. These include: a shirt with sleeves, shorts, shin pads covered by straps, and boots. It has to be stated that the area of boots is arbitrary, in that any footwear is permitted that, in the referee's opinion, does not pose a threat to the player or any of his fellow players or opponents. Key to underwear and vests is that they are of a uniform nature to the rest of the kit, i.e. they have to be of the same colour as the rest of the kit. When a player has just scored, he becomes possessed by an unswerving desire to rip his jersey from his torso. This behaviour will usually earn him a yellow card. The most important rule on shirts, of course, is that both teams need to be kitted out in a noticeably distinct colour. Nonetheless, there have been some notable slip-ups in the past. At the World Cup in 1978 in Argentina, for example, Hungary and France both wanted to wear white. This was not the fault of the kit managers, but that of an official. Both teams had actually been instructed to play in white. Replacement kit had to be fetched from local Argentine club Atlético Kimberley and France went on to beat Hungary 3–2 wearing Atlético's green and white vests in a late kick-off.

Exchanging Shirts

Swapping shirts is a popular ritual usually performed at the end of a very important football match. Arguments sometimes flare up among team mates over which one them will swap shirts with an opposing global superstar such as Ronaldo or Messi. Young players should take note: a half-time shirt exchange is an awful faux pas likely to land you in hot water with the gaffer, the TV pundits and, most importantly, your own fans.

It is chronicled in FIFA that the first football shirt-swap came about on 14 May 1931, when players of the French national side asked the English players they had just beaten 5–2 for their shirts. Socially acceptable? We think not.

What was truly acceptable was the gesture shown following Brazil's 1–0 victory over England at the World Cup of 1970 when two great legends of the game exchanged shirts – Brazilian Pelé and Englishman Bobby Moore. One of football's great images that will forever be engraved on our collective memories.

A Numbers Game

Actually having numbers on football shirts was premiered at the FA Cup final of 1933 in England. On that day, the Everton players pitched up with the numbers 1 to 11 on their backs and their opponents, Manchester City, wore 12 to 22. Later, numbers were assigned for certain playing positions. Even now, goalkeepers still wear the number 1. However, since many teams use two number 6 players in front of their defence the whole idea of assigning numbers to positions on the field has become confusing. By the time of the 1978 World Cup, the Argentine coach, Menotti, was so fed up with his players squabbling over shirt numbers he ordered them to simply use the numbers in alphabetical order according to their names. It was a good shout. His team went on to win it. By dint of his surname, number 22 in that squad was Spurs legend Ricky Villa. When he played in the FA Cup Final three years later, Villa wore number 6. As number 22, he had not made it onto the pitch in Buenos Aires, but as 6, he scored a brace including the winner in the replay against Manchester City at Wembley.

Fixture List (or Match Programme)

A favoured pastime of all football fans is shoptalk. And the basis for that is supplied by the statistics. The most important one of those of course is the league table, which the soccer devotee will spend hours studying, especially when his own team is doing well. Our book is packed with statistics. There is important data on each national team including its FIFA code, its position in the FIFA world rankings (taken 1 December 2017), as well the year the national football association was established. Special mention is given to the player with the most caps for his country, and the all-time top scorer. There is additional information on whether each country has a national women's team, the kit manufacturer/designer, and what the highest wins and defeats are. And lastly, there are many interesting and amusing football anecdotes for each country to keep everyone talking. This lot should keep you busy until the next big tournament.

Michael Brepohl

THE
TEAMS

Asian Football Confederation

The Asian football associations are controlled by the Asian Football Confederation. Forty-seven national associations constitute this organisation, which was founded in Manila, Philippines, in 1954. Its most prestigious competition is the AFC Asian Cup, also known as the Asian Football Championships. Some countries do not join continental associations according to where they are located, rather their decision is more influenced by sporting considerations. This would explain why Australia switched from the Oceania Football Confederation (OFC). Those responsible 'down under' saw membership of the AFC as a better opportunity to net one of the coveted places in the World Cup qualification.

AFGHANISTAN / AFC

147th (181 points) ⇅

🏳 Afghanistan Football Federation

❄ 1933
. . . .
👤 Zohib Islam Amiri (42)
. . . .
⚽ Belal Arezou (9)
. . . .
👤 Yes
. . . .
👟 Hummel
. . . .
📱 **Biggest Win**
Bhutan 1–8 Afghanistan
(7 December 2011)

Biggest Defeat
Turkmenistan 11–0 Afghanistan
(19 November 2003)

Competitive Records 🏆

World Cup Never qualified

Asian Cup Never qualified
. . . .
Current Results

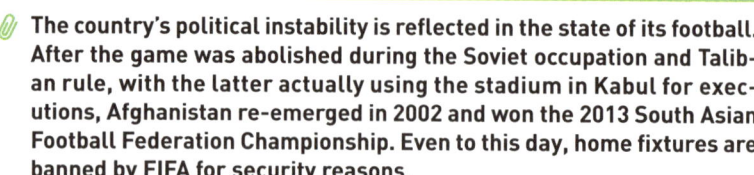

📎 The country's political instability is reflected in the state of its football. After the game was abolished during the Soviet occupation and Taliban rule, with the latter actually using the stadium in Kabul for executions, Afghanistan re-emerged in 2002 and won the 2013 South Asian Football Federation Championship. Even to this day, home fixtures are banned by FIFA for security reasons.

AUSTRALIA / AFC

FOOTBALL FEDERATION AUSTRALIA

39th (747 points) ↕

Football Federation Australia

1961

Mark Schwarzer (109)

Tim Cahill (50)

Yes

Nike

Biggest Win
Australia 31–0 American Samoa
(11 April 2001)

Biggest Defeat
Australia 0–8 South Africa
(17 September 1955)

Competitive Records

World Cup Appearances 4
Round of 16 2006
Qualified for 2018*

Asian Cup Appearances 3
Champions 2015

Current Results

Germany 2006. The quarter-final game against Italy. The Australian national team had never gone so far in a World Cup finals before. The Socceroos had been holding firm. With the 90th minute up, five more were added on. In the 95th minute the ref blew. Penalty for Italy. Australia were out. They still secured themselves a place in the record books though – a spot kick had never been given so late in a World Cup finals game before.

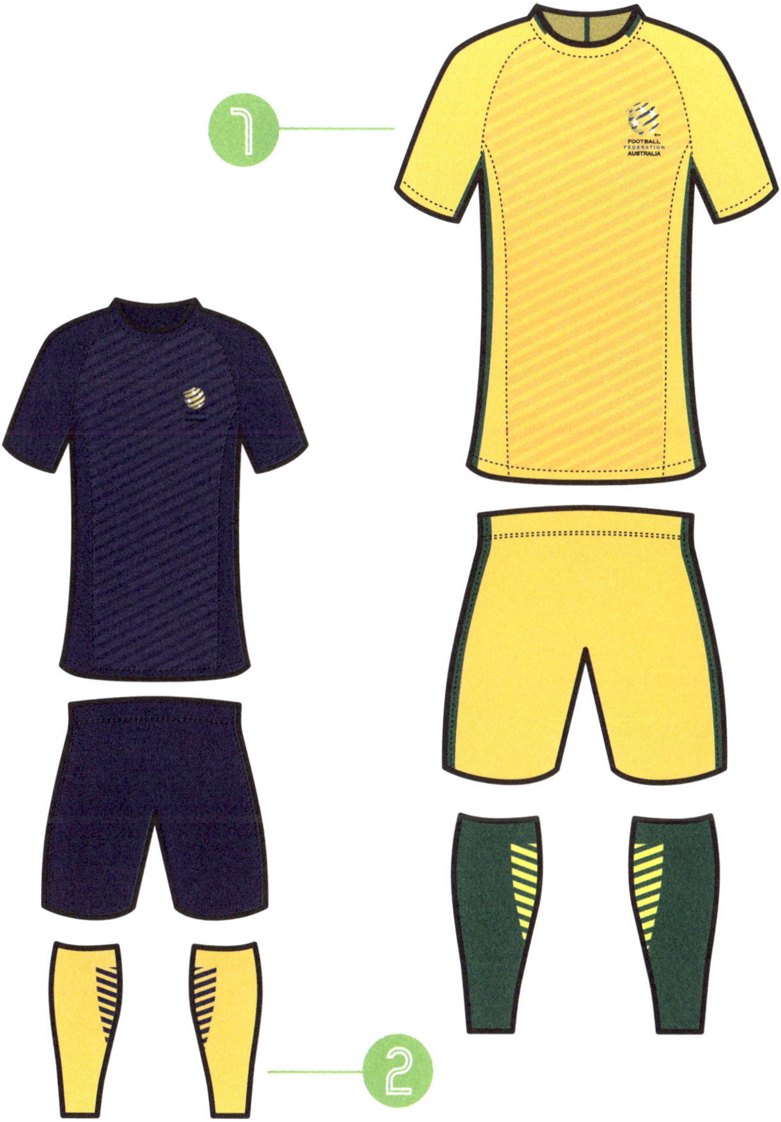

* Kit as far as known 3 January 2018

BANGLADESH / AFC

192nd (38 points) ⇅

🏳 **Bangladesh Football Federation**

✳ 1972

👤 Rajani Kanta Barman (48)

⚽ Sheikh Mohammad Aslam (38)

👤 Yes

🚌 -

🖩 **Biggest Win**
Bangladesh 8–0 Maldives
(21 December 1985)

Biggest Defeat
South Korea 9–0 Bangladesh (16 September 1979); Iran 9–0 Bangladesh
(25 February 1982)

Competitive Records 🏆

World Cup Never qualified

Asian Cup Appearances 1
Group stage 1980

Current Results

📎 **This is not a country where footballing success stories are mass produced, unless you're talking about shirts. Bangladesh is home to the production of most of the top teams' kits. Although the fact that the local seamstresses work in poor conditions and take home less than ten pence per shirt makes many want to show those responsible the red card.**

BAHRAIN / AFC

115th (282 points)

🚩 al-Ittihad al-bahraini li-kurat al-qadam

☀ 1957

👤 Salman Isa (156)

⚽ Ismail Abdul-Latif (34)

👤 Yes

🚌 Puma

📇 **Biggest Win**
Bahrain 10–0 Indonesia
(29 February 2012)

Biggest Defeat
Iraq 10–1 Bahrain
(7 April 1966)

🏆 Competitive Records

World Cup Never qualified

Asian Cup Appearances 5
Fourth place 2004

Current Results

📎 **A'ala Hubail** and the **Golden Boot** sounds like a tale from *Arabian Nights* but it was, in fact, the reward given to the prolific striker for his five goals at the 2004 AFC Asian Cup in China. Even though they narrowly missed out against Japan in the semi-final, at least one Bahraini player was able to raise a trophy in the air. But not for long, as he was banged up five years later for taking part in anti-government protests.

1

2

BHUTAN / AFC

185th (55 points)

⌑ Bhutan Football Federation

1983
....
👤 Chencho Gyeltshen (26)
....
⚽ Chencho Gyeltshen (9)
....
👤 Yes
....
🚌 FBT
....

Biggest Win
Bhutan 6–0 Guam
(23 April 2003)

Biggest Defeat
Kuwait 20–0 Bhutan
(14 February 2000)

Competitive Records 🏆

World Cup Never qualified

Asian Cup Never qualified
....

Current Results

📎 In step with its Buddhist values, there is a special state commission in Bhutan that measures the gross domestic happiness of the country. Its national football team is certainly not a major contributor. They traditionally lose, except the once, when they played against Montserrat in 2002 (who were last in the FIFA rankings). In front of the cameras and a packed house, Bhutan contrived to beat their lowly rivals 4–0. So, they didn't even get the wooden spoon, which might have come in handy to stir the Ema Datshi (delicious national dish of cheese and chillies).

BRUNEI / AFC

⊕

190th (45 points)   ⇅

⚑ National Football Association of Brunei Darussalam

✳ 1952

⚇ Azwan Saleh (26)

🎯 Shahrazen Said (8)

⚇ -

🚗 -

▦ **Biggest Win**
Brunei 4–0 East Timor
(2 November 2016)

Biggest Defeat
Brunei 0–12 United Arab Emirates
(14 April 2001)

Competitive Records   🏆

World Cup Never qualified

Asian Cup Never qualified

Current Results

✎

📎 **The Sultan of Brunei is one of the richest people in the world, but football is not one of his passions. The meagre status of the national team would seem to point in that direction anyway. Sixty years after being set up, the team boasts only eight wins and no appearances at major competitions.**

CAMBODIA / AFC

170th (98 points)

🏳 Football Federation of Cambodia

✳ 1933

👤 Hok Sochetra (42)

🔫 Kouch Sokumpheak (43)

👤 -

🚗 FBT

🧮 **Biggest Win**
Cambodia 11–0 North Yemen
(29 November 1966)

Biggest Defeat
Indonesia 10–0 Cambodia
(6 September 1995)

Competitive Records

World Cup Never qualified

Asian Cup Appearances 1
Fourth place 1972

Current Results

Cambodia was trotting along quite nicely, with wins over more fancied rivals such as Japan and China, when the Khmer Rouge's reign of terror broke out. After many years of oppression, the country is now gradually recovering but, judging from its teams FIFA world ranking, its football is not. Cambodia are propping up the charts.

CHINA / AFC

60th (561 points)

🏳 **Chinese Football Association**

✳ 1924

👤 Li Weifeng (112)

🎯 Hao Haidong (41)

👤 Yes

👟 Nike

🖩 **Biggest Win**
China 19–0 Guam
(26 January 2000)

Biggest Defeat
Brazil 8–0 China
(10 September 2012)

Competitive Records 🏆

World Cup Appearances 1
Group stage 2002

Asian Cup Appearances 12
Runners-up 1984, 2004

Current Results

Confucius said: 'People do not stumble over mountains, but over molehills.' This was the case for China in 1982 when Kuwait and New Zealand stopped them from making it to the World Cup finals. Twenty years on and they were finally there, only to be knocked out of the competition by Costa Rica, Turkey and Brazil without scoring a single goal. In World Cup history, only four other teams have managed this dubious feat. Can you name them?

GUAM / AFC

191st (43 points) ⇅

🏳 Guam Football Association

✳ 1975

👤 Jason Cunliffe (40)

🔫 Jason Cunliffe (12)

👤 Yes

🚙 Adidas

📅 **Biggest Win**
Palau 2–15 Guam
(1 August 1998)

Biggest Defeat
Guam 0–21 North Korea
(11 March 2005)

Competitive Records 🏆

World Cup Never qualified

Asian Cup Never qualified

Current Results

📎 **Long before Kim Jong-un's threats catapulted this West Pacific island nation into the limelight, it had already suffered a frightening defeat on the football field. In 2008, Guam were defeated 21–0 by North Korea. Hopefully, these nations will not clash again, on or off the field.**

HONG KONG / AFC

143rd (189 points) ⇅

⚑ The Hong Kong Football Association

✳ 1914

👤 Lee Chi Ho (70)

🏹 Chan Siu Ki (40)

👤 Yes

👟 Nike

🖩 **Biggest Win**
Hong Kong 15–0 Guam
(7 March 2005)

Biggest Defeat
Hong Kong 0–7 Argentina
(14 October 2014)

Competitive Records 🏆

World Cup Never qualified

Asian Cup Appearances 3
Third place 1956

Current Results

Strictly speaking, it is difficult to discuss a national team in the case of Hong Kong. The talk nowadays should rather be about a Special Administrative Region of China. Since 1997, the former British Crown Colony has been nothing more than that. The 'one country, two systems' policy promulgated by China has proven unsuccessful when applied to football. In fact, neither system has achieved any noteworthy success so far. QPR fans will be delighted to note that local hero Tony Sealy's son, Jack, has run out on occasion for the Dragons.

INDONESIA / AFC

154th (144 points) ⇅

🚩 Football Association of Indonesia

✳ 1930

👤 Bambang Pamungkas (86)

⚽ Soetjipto Soentoro (57)

👤 -

👟 Nike

🗓 **Biggest Win**
Indonesia 12–0 Philippines (21
September 1972); Indonesia 13–1
Philippines (23 December 2002)

Biggest Defeat
Bahrain 10–0 Indonesia
(29 February 2012)

Competitive Records 🏆

World Cup Appearances 1
Round 1 1938

Asian Cup Appearances 4
Group stage 1996, 2000, 2004, 2007

Current Results

As the world's fourth most populous nation, Indonesia is no stranger to impressive numbers. In 2002, no fewer than 100,000 spectators attended the finals of the ASEAN football championship, or Tiger Cup, as it was known, in Jakarta, only to see their side lose to Thailand on penalties. Indonesia reached the final again in 2004. Over 110,000 watched them go down 3–1 at home to neighbours Singapore. That kind of popularity is something other big teams can only dream of, which ironically now also includes the Indonesians, because the Gelora Bung Karno stadium recently had its capacity reduced to just 80,000 seats.

INDIA / AFC

105th (320 points) ⇅

🏳 **All India Football Federation**

✳ 1937

👤 Sunil Chhetri (102)

⚽ Sunil Chhetri (55)

👤 Yes

👟 Nike

🧮 **Biggest Win**
India 6–0 Cambodia
(17 August 2007)

Biggest Defeat
Soviet Union 11–1 India
(16 September 1955)

🏆 **Competitive Records**

World Cup Never qualified

Asian Cup Appearances 3
Runners-up 1964

Current Results

📎 **India were invited to the 1950 World Cup in Brazil but they declined. There is an array of myths surrounding the reasoning behind their decision. It is rumoured that India did not want to play wearing football boots (FIFA had just banned playing barefoot). The national team did adopt boots a short time later and almost won a bronze medal at the Melbourne Olympic Games in 1956 as a result. With the likes of Marco Materazzi, Teddy Sheringham, David James, Steve Coppell and Roberto Carlos lending their considerable expertise to the Indian Super League, football on the subcontinent is looking up.**

IRAN / AFC

🌐

32nd (798 points) ⇅

🏳 Football Federation Islamic Republic of Iran

✳ 1920

👤 Javad Nekounam (151)

⚽ Ali Daei (109)

👤 Yes

👟 Adidas

🗓 **Biggest Win**
Iran 19–0 Guam
(24 November 2000)

Biggest Defeat
Turkey 6–1 Iran (28 May 1950);
South Korea 5–0 Iran (28 May 1958)

Competitive Records 🏆

World Cup Appearances 5
(First) group stage 1978, 1998, 2006, 2014
Qualified for 2018*

Asian Cup Appearances 14
Champions 1968, 1972, 1976

Current Results ✏

📎 The Iranian national team, known as the 'Tim-i Melli', are one of the best teams in Asia. In addition to four World Cup finals appearances, they have won the Asian Cup three times in a row. Iran would surely have been even more successful had political conflicts and government interference not interrupted their progress.

* Kit as far as known 3 January 2018

IRAQ / AFC

79th (438 points)

⚑ al-Ittihad al-'iraqi li-kurat al-qadam

✳ 1948

👤 Yunis Mahmud (148)

🎯 Hussain Said (78)

👤 Yes

🚌 Jako

📅 **Biggest Win**
Iraq 13–0 Ethiopia
(18 August 1992)

Biggest Defeat
Chile 6–0 Iraq
(14 August 2013)

🏆 Competitive Records

World Cup Appearances 1
Group stage 1986

Asian Cup Appearances 8
Champions 2007

Current Results

📎 **Home advantage is completely irrelevant to Iraqi football fans. Due to war and conflict, the national team has been forced to play its home matches abroad for more than three decades. Despite not really playing at home, the team has nevertheless enjoyed moderate success, including the Asian Cup win in 2007, which is commemorated by a monument on the road to the Al-Shaab Stadium in Baghdad not far from Firdos Square where the statue of Saddam Hussein was toppled in 2003.**

JORDAN / AFC

107th (311 points)

🏳 Jordan Football Association

※ 1949

👤 Amer Shafi (141)

⚽ Hassan Abdel Fattah Mahmoud (30)

👤 Yes

👟 Adidas

🖩 **Biggest Win**
Jordan 9–0 Nepal
(23 July 2011)

Biggest Defeat
Japan 6–0 Jordan
(8 June 2012)

Competitive Records

World Cup Never qualified

Asian Cup Appearances 3
Quarter-finals 2004, 2011

Current Results

📎 **Everyone who puts on a pair of football boots dreams of one day scoring a decisive goal for his team. Such reverie has become reality for Hassan Abdel Fattah on numerous occasions. The Jordanian superstar scored in the sensational 1–1 draw with Japan, got both goals in the 2–2 draw against South Korea, and then hit four in his country's record win over Nepal.**

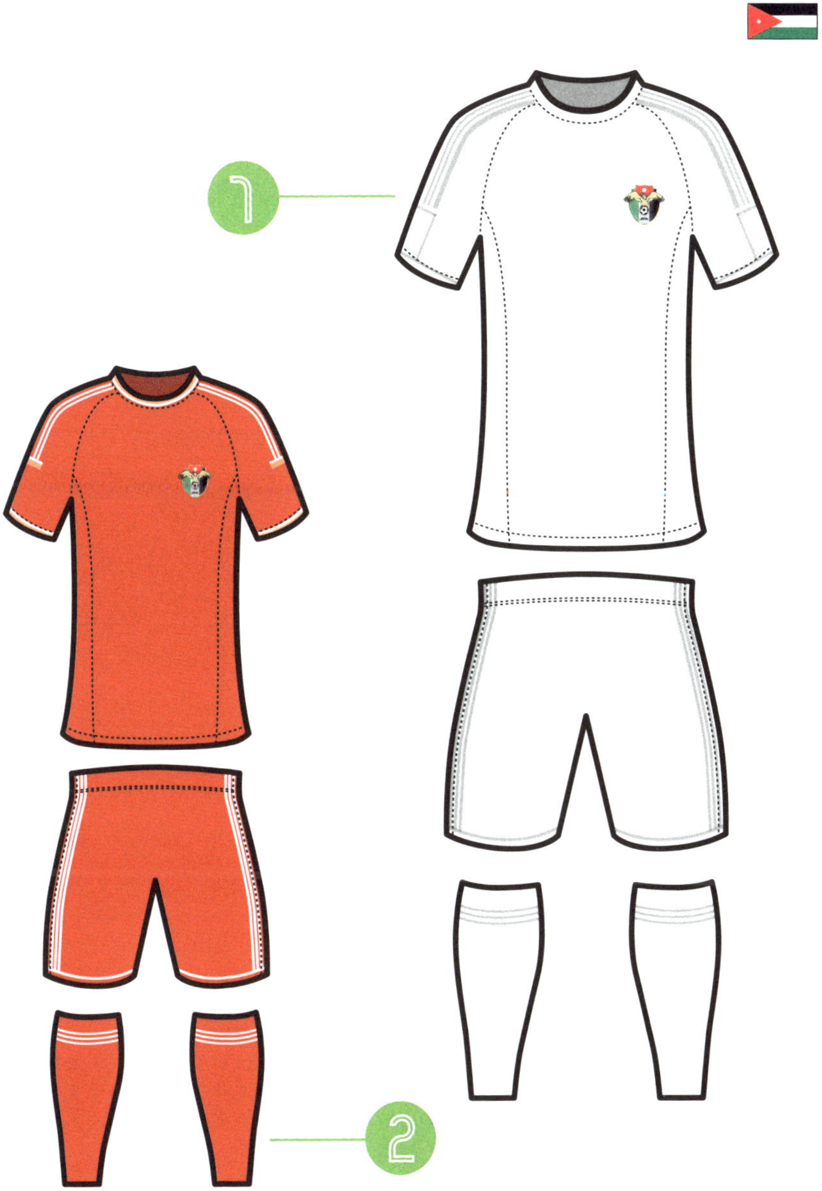

1

2

JAPAN / AFC

55th (623 points) ↑↓

⚑ Japan Football Association

✳ 1921

👤 Yasuhito Endō (152)

🔫 Kunishige Kamamoto (80)

👤 Yes

👟 Adidas

🧮 **Biggest Win**
Japan 15–0 Philippines
(27 September 1967)

Biggest Defeat
Japan 2–15 Philippines
(10 September 1917)

🏆 Competitive Records

World Cup Appearances 6
Round of 16 2002, 2010
Qualified for 2018*

Asian Cup Appearances 8
Champions 1992, 2000, 2004, 2011

Current Results

📎 **The warrior dramas of Japanese Noh theatre never end well, which is a little akin to the game the Japanese team played against Iraq in Qatar in 1993. With five minutes left to play, Japan were 2–1 up and looked to have booked their ticket for the 1994 World Cup finals in the United States. But, by the 92nd minute, Omran scored from a corner and the ref blew for time. The South Koreans still celebrate it as the Miracle of Doha. In Japan, they act out its tragic scenes as the Agony of Doha.**

* Kit as far as known 3 January 2018

KYRGYZSTAN / AFC

FFKR

115th (282 points) ↑↓

⚑ Football Federation of Kyrgyz Republic

❋ 1992

👤 Wadim Chartschenko (54)

⚽ Anton Semljanuchin (7)

👤 -

🚚 Adidas

📅 **Biggest Win**
Kyrgyzstan 6–0 Maldives
(13 June 1997)

Biggest Defeat
Iran 7–0 Kyrgyzstan
(4 June 1997)

Competitive Records 🏆

World Cup Never qualified

Asian Cup Never qualified

Current Results

The name of the Spartak stadium in Bishkek reveals a lot about history. It summons up impressions of the country's association with the former Soviet Union, which in turn saw itself as a champion in the image of the Roman gladiator Spartacus. As for the national team, there is a very low attraction to football and the Kyrgyz team has done little to change that. However, in the tradition of Spartacus, Kyrgyz athletes won medals for Greco-Roman wrestling at the Beijing Olympics in 2008.

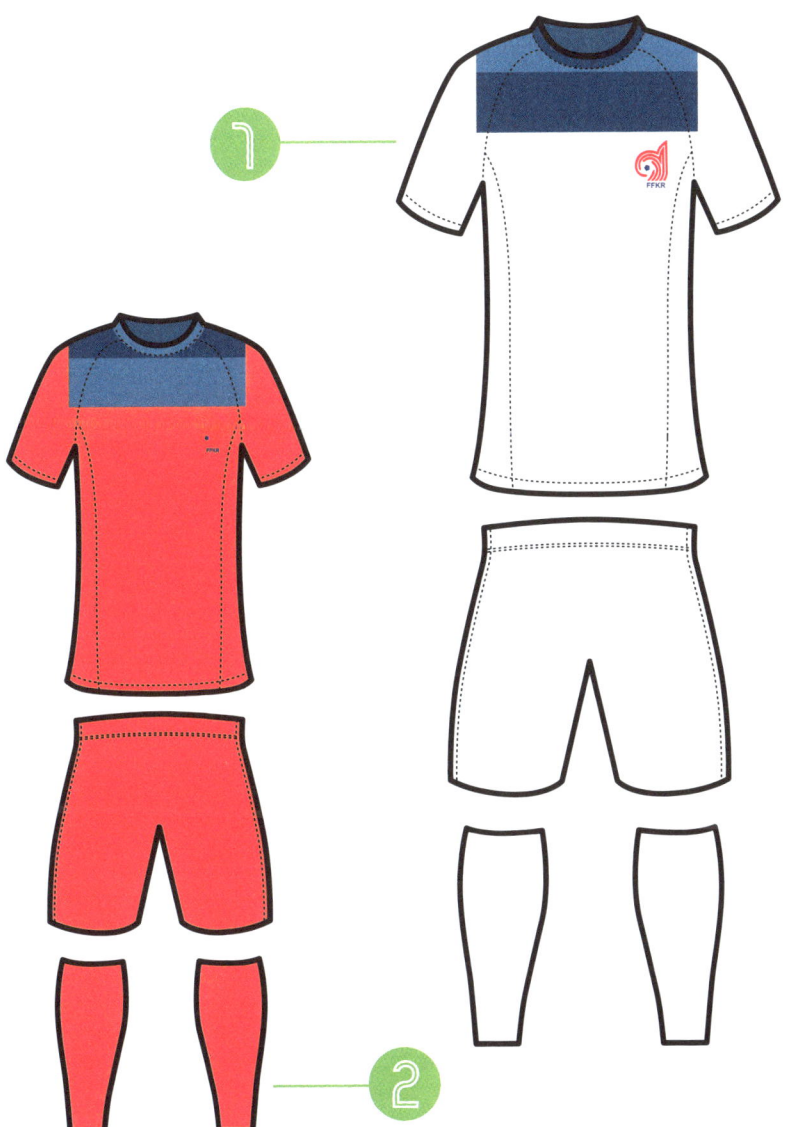

SOUTH KOREA / AFC

59th (563 points)

🏳 Korea Football Association

✳ 1928

👤 Hong Myung-bo (136)

⚽ Cha Bum-kun (57)

👤 Yes

👟 Nike

🖩 **Biggest Win**
South Korea 16–0 Nepal
(29 September 2003)

Biggest Defeat
Sweden 12–0 South Korea
(5 August 1948)

🏆 **Competitive Records**

World Cup Appearances 10
Fourth place 2002
Qualified for 2018*

Asian Cup Appearances 13
Champions 1956, 1960

Current Results

📎 The reason South Korea are a strong force in football is largely down to ball games having such a long-standing tradition in the country. Before the end of the 19th century, when football was unknown, the South Koreans played a traditional game called 'chuk-guk', which was remarkably similar to modern day football. In 2002, South Korea reached the semi-finals in their own country. That aside, they have previously qualified for a number of World Cups. In case you were wondering, half the population shares just three surnames, which is why so many players are called Kim, Park and Lee.

* Kit as far as known 3 January 2018

SAUDI ARABIA / AFC

63rd (539 points)

🏳 Saudi Arabia Football Federation

✳ 1959

👤 Mohamed Al-Deayea (178)

🔫 Madschid Abdullah (71)

👤 -

👟 Nike

📅 **Biggest Win**
East Timor 0–10 Saudi Arabia
(17 November 2015)

Biggest Defeat
Egypt 13–0 Saudi Arabia
(3 September 1961)

Competitive Records 🏆

World Cup Appearances 5
Rounds of 16 1994
Qualified for 2018*

Asian Cup Appearances 9
Champions 1984, 1988, 1996

Current Results

📎 **The ban on women's football was eased in 2006. At the first Women's Championship in 2008, men were not allowed in the stadium. Football is extremely popular here and the Saudi men's team have already achieved international success. They have qualified for four World Cup finals and they became the first Asian team to make it to the round of 16 in the US in 1994.**

KUWAIT / AFC

188th (52 points) ⇅

🏳 Kuwait Football Association

✳ 1952

👤 Bader Al-Mutawa (156)

🔫 Bashar Abdullah (75)

👤 -

👟 Puma

🖩 **Biggest Win**
Kuwait 20–0 Bhutan
(14 February 2000)

Biggest Defeat
Portugal 8–0 Kuwait
(19 November 2003)

Competitive Records 🏆

World Cup Appearances 1
First group stage 1982

Asian Cup Appearances 10
Champions 1980

Current Results

🖉

This has to be one of the biggest World Cup scandals ever. In 1982, when playing against France, the Kuwaiti team suddenly appeared to be fielding one player too many on the pitch. Sheikh Fahid al-Ahmad al Sabah demanded that the referee disqualify France's fourth goal. He claimed that his team had been agitated by the crowd. To the amazement of all, the goal was indeed ruled out, but Kuwait still lost 4–1.

LAOS / AFC

🌐

184th (62 points) ⇅

🏳 Fédération Lao de Football

✳ 1951
....
👤 Visay Phaphouvanin (51)
....
👟 Visay Phaphouvanin (18)
....
👤 -
....
🚌 FBT
....

📋 **Biggest Win**
Laos 6–1 East Timor
(26 October 2010)

Biggest Defeat
Egypt 15–0 Laos
(12 December 1961)

Competitive Records 🏆

World Cup Never qualified

Asian Cup Never qualified
....
Current Results

🖊

📎 **One of the principles of Buddhism is to abstain from intoxicating substances, which could be the best explanation for the Lao national team's lack of intoxicating success and their status as one of the worst national teams in the world. Laos have only ever qualified for the group stage of a tournament once and that was down to two other teams pulling out.**

LEBANON / AFC

87th (404 points) ↑↓

🏴 Fédération Libanaise de Football Association

✳ 1933

👤 Abbas Ahmed Atwi (84)

⚽ Roda Antar (20)

👤 -

🚌 Capelli Sport

🖩 **Biggest Win**
Lebanon 11–0 Afghanistan
(5 October 2002)

Biggest Defeat
Qatar 8–0 Lebanon
(27 March 1985)

Competitive Records 🏆

World Cup Never qualified

Asian Cup Appearances 2
Group stage 2000

Current Results

📎 Football often feasts upon a rhetoric of warlike proportions. Gerd Müller, for example, was known as 'Der Bomber' (I say Gerd Müller because only West Brom fans will remember Tony 'Bomber' Brown and you'd probably have to have a telegram from the Queen to remember Huddersfield's George 'Bomber' Brown). But, take the case of Lebanon in 2006 – they had to pull out of the Asian Games because Beirut airport was being bombarded during the conflict between Israel and Hezbollah. This made flying into the country for away teams impossible.

MACAU / AFC

182nd (65 points)

⚑ Associação de Futebol de Macau

❉ 1939

👤 Cheang Cheng leong (44)

⚽ Chan Kin Seng (17)

👤 -

👟 Nike

🧮 **Biggest Win**
Macau 5–1 Philippines
(4 February 1996)

Biggest Defeat
Japan 10–0 Macau
(22 June 1997)

Competitive Records 🏆

World Cup Never qualified

Asian Cup Never qualified

Current Results

📎 The former Portuguese colony, and today's 'Special Administrative Region of the People's Republic of China', is the Las Vegas of Asia. But not all bets are legal. During the last World Cup in Brazil, a betting ring that had illegally wagered 474 million dollars was captured. It is probably a bad idea to place a bet on Macau itself because the team loses too often.

MALAYSIA / AFC

174th (97 points) ⇅

⚑ Football Association of Malaysia

✳ 1933

👤 R. Arumugam (196)

⚽ Mokhtar Dahari (125)

👤 Yes

👟 Nike

🖩 **Biggest Win**
Malaysia 15–1 Philippines
(26 August 1962)

Biggest Defeat
Malaysia 0–11 PR China
(20 December 1978)

Competitive Records 🏆

World Cup Never qualified

Asian Cup Appearances 3
Group stage 1976, 1980, 2007

Current Results

📎 **Some teams seem to always draw the short straw. After the national team qualified for the Moscow Olympics in 1980, their government decided to join in the boycott of the games, leaving the 2010 Southeast Asia Games as the only success Malaysia has to shout about so far.**

1

2

MALDIVES / AFC

157th (135 points)

🏳 Football Association of Maldives

❇ 1982

👤 Imran Mohamed (95)

🔫 Ali Ashfaq (52)

👤 Yes

👟 Joma

📅 **Biggest Win**
Maldives 12–0 Mongolia
(3 December 2003)

Biggest Defeat
Maldives 0–17 Iran
(2 June 1997)

Competitive Records 🏆

World Cup Never qualified

Asian Cup Never qualified

Current Results

In 2008, the Maldives hosted the South Asian Cup, but it is doubtful whether further tournaments will ever be held here in the future. Climate change could cause their 1,196 islands to disappear into the sea. They did go on to win the tournament held on their own soil, which is the national team's first and only title so far.

MONGOLIA / AFC

199th (17 points) ↕

🏳 Mongolian Football Federation

❄ 1959

👤 Donorowyn Lübmengaraw (35)

🔫 Donorowyn Lübmengaraw (8)

👤 -

🚐 Adidas

🗓 **Biggest Win**
Northern Mariana Islands 0–8
Mongolia (4 July 2016)

Biggest Defeat
Uzbekistan 15–0 Mongolia
(5 December 1998)

Competitive Records 🏆

World Cup Never qualified

Asian Cup Never qualified

Current Results

🖊

📎 'A man's greatest pleasure is to defeat his enemy,' Genghis Khan once said, and the spirit with which the Mongol ruler brought half the world under his fist does not seem to have got through to the Mongolian national team. Their successes can virtually be counted on one hand and so far they have only been victorious against lightweights such as Guam and Macao.

MYANMAR / AFC

150th (176 points)

Myanmar Football Federation

1947

Myo Hlaing Win (90)

Myo Hlaing Win (39)

Yes

FBT

Biggest Win
Myanmar 9–0 Singapore
(9 November 1969)

Biggest Defeat
Kuwait 9–0 Myanmar
(3 September 2015)

Competitive Records

World Cup Never qualified

Asian Cup Appearances 1
Runners-up 1968

Current Results

Many Asians will remember Suk Bahadur, the Gurkha, and his great Burma team of the 1960s. But Myanmar is a mainly Buddhist country and Buddhists are considered to be an especially peace-loving people. Astonishingly though, their team were disqualified from the 2018 World Cup due to the violence of their fans. As it stands, they are eligible to play again, but only at neutral venues, and are still banned from competing at home.

NEPAL / AFC

170th (98 points)

🏳 All Nepal Football Association

* 1951
....

👤 Nawayug Shrestha (12)
....

Biraj Maharjan (59)
....

👤 Yes
....

 Adidas
....

🖩 **Biggest Win**
Nepal 7–0 Bhutan
(26 September 1999)

Biggest Defeat
South Korea 16–0 Nepal
(29 September 2003)

🏆 Competitive Records

World Cup Never qualified

Asian Cup Never qualified
....

Current Results

'Give up trying to win, just find happiness.' The Nepalese observe, for the main part, the teachings of Buddha, who is said to have been born here. They must have lost track somewhere though, because in the 1993 South Asian Games they won in a penalty shoot-out against much stronger Indian opposition. They certainly gained much happiness from that win.

OMAN / AFC

101st (350 points) ⇅

🏳 Oman Football Association

✳ 1978

👤 Fawzi Bashir (143)

🥅 Hani Al-Dhabit (42)

👤 -

👟 Kappa

🧮 **Biggest Win**
Oman 14–0 Bhutan
(28 March 2017)

Biggest Defeat
Libya 21–0 Oman
(1 April 1966)

Competitive Records 🏆

World Cup Never qualified

Asian Cup Appearances 4
Group stage 2004, 2007

Current Results

🖉

📎 **It was a bumpy start for Oman. After their first ever international game in 1965, which they lost, the team would need another 20 years before they could celebrate their first win. That came about in 1986 when they comprehensively thumped Nepal 8–0. Oman seemed to get a taste for winning and they went on to beat South Korea. The Omanis also secured their first Gulf Cup of Nations not long after.**

PAKISTAN / AFC

PAKISTAN FOOTBALL FEDERATION

201st (15 points)

⚐ Pakistan Football Federation

❋ 1947

👤 Jaffar Khan (43)

⚽ Muhammad Essa (20)

👤 -

👕 Forward Sports

🖩 **Biggest Win**
Pakistan 9–2 Guam
(6 April 2008)

Biggest Defeat
Iran 9–1 Pakistan
(21 March 1969)

Competitive Records 🏆

World Cup Never qualified

Asian Cup Never qualified

Current Results

📎 **Pakistan won the World Cup in 1992 and were runners-up in 1999. Whilst they may be cricketing wizards, however, football very much plays second fiddle. The national football side has always been eliminated early from the few qualifying competitions it has taken part in. Pakistan does still play a major role on all the football pitches of the world. The city of Sialkot in the Punjab is home to the production of over 40 million football kits every year and production has been known to rise to 60 million when there is a major tournament on.**

PHILIPPINES / AFC

118th (280 points)

Philippine Football Federation

✳ 1907

👤 Phil Younghusband (91)

➹ Phil Younghusband (47)

👤 Yes

🚌 LGR

🧮 **Biggest Win**
Japan 2–15 Philippines
(10 September 1917)

Biggest Defeat
Japan 15–0 Philippines
(27 September 1967)

Competitive Records 🏆

World Cup Never qualified

Asian Cup Never qualified

Current Results

Imelda Marcos, wife of the famous Philippines dictator, Ferdinand, is said to have owned the world's largest collection of shoes. Whether she kept footy boots among them is another matter. Interest in football in this country, made up of 7,107 islands, is very limited and the national team is not particularly successful. It is, therefore, highly unlikely that Mrs Marcos kept a pair of Adidas Predators next to her Christian Louboutins.

PALESTINE / AFC

82nd (427 points)   ↕

⚑ Palestinian Football Association

✳ 1962

👤 Ramzi Saleh (68)

🏹 Fahed Attal (15)

👤 Yes

👟 Peak

🖩 **Biggest Win**
Palestine 11–0 Guam
(1 April 2006)

Biggest Defeat
Egypt 8–1 Palestine (26 July 1953);
Iran 7–0 Palestine (5 October 2011)

Competitive Records 🏆

World Cup Never qualified

Asian Cup Appearances 2
Group stage 2015

Current Results

📎 **The conflict in the Middle East** means very little happens on the football pitches in this country. Games are forever being cancelled because of hostilities in Gaza or the West Bank, often at the very last minute too. Several international players have been killed as a result of bombing raids, which means Palestinian football is probably something best left unaddressed in this book.

NORTH KOREA / AFC

114th (283 points)

⌕ DPR Korea Football Association

✳ 1945

⚇ Ri Myong-guk (90)

⚽ Jong Tae-se (15)

⚇ -

🚍 Legea

🖩 **Biggest Win**
North Korea 21–0 Guam
(11 March 2005)

Biggest Defeat
Portugal 7–0 North Korea
(21 June 2010)

Competitive Records 🏆

World Cup Appearances 2
Quarter-finals 1966

Asian Cup Appearances 4
Fourth place 1980

Current Results

📎 **The North Korean media hide anything that could in any way give a bad impression of the country. Football matches, therefore, tend not to be broadcast live. In 2010, the national team, considered hopelessly inferior to Brazil, played exceptionally well and narrowly lost 2–1. As a result, their next game against Portugal was shown live. The North Koreans contrived to lose it 7–0. It was their last live broadcast for a long time.**

QATAR / AFC

102nd (336 points) ↑↓

🏳 Qatar Football Association

✳ 1960

👤 Sebastián Soria (123)

🔫 Sebastián Soria (40)

👤 -

👟 Nike

🧮 **Biggest Win**
Qatar 15–0 Bhutan
(3 September 2015)

Biggest Defeat
Kuwait 9–0 Qatar
(8 January 1973)

Competitive Records 🏆

World Cup Never qualified

Asian Cup Appearances 10
Quarter-finals 2000, 2011

Current Results

📎 **Alcohol is frowned upon in the Arabian peninsula, so it is quite surprising that the national team is known as the 'al-Anabbi' or the 'Red Wines'. This is by no means the only controversy surrounding Qatari soccer. Events leading to the country being named host for the 2022 World Cup have also cast a shadow over this gas- and oil-rich Emirate.**

SINGAPORE / AFC

170th (98 points)

🏳 Football Association of Singapore

✳ 1892

👤 Daniel Bennett (135)

⚽ Fandi Ahmad (55)

👤 Yes

👟 Nike

🗒 **Biggest Win**
Singapore 11–0 Laos
(15 January 2007)

Biggest Defeat
Myanmar 9–0 Singapore
(9 November 1969)

Competitive Records 🏆

World Cup Never qualified

Asian Cup Appearances 1
Group stage 1984

Current Results

📎 **One of the ugliest things we can see on a football field, particularly if children are watching, is when a player spits in front of the camera. In the home of the four-time South East Asian champions, it is best to avoid this bad habit altogether. There is a four-figure fine for such improper conduct. El Hadji Diouf had better watch his manners if he ever finds himself in the Lion City.**

SRI LANKA / AFC

FFSL

200th (16 points) ⇅

🏳 **Football Federation of Sri Lanka**

✳ 1939
....

👤 Dumidu Hettiarachchi (24)
....

🏹 Kasun Jayasuriya (27)
....

👤 Yes
....

👕 Grand Sport
....

🖩 **Biggest Win**
Sri Lanka 6–0 Bhutan
(6 December 2009)

Biggest Defeat
Ceylon 1–12 East Germany
(12 January 1964)

Competitive Records 🏆

World Cup Never qualified

Asian Cup Never qualified
....

Current Results

🖊

📎 **Sri Lanka won the World Cup in 1996. Unfortunately, for their footballers, the discipline was cricket. The football team have never qualified for a football World Cup, although they came very close for the most recent one. Ultimately, they were defeated by Bhutan, a team thankful for a little bit of extra cash to boost their meagre monthly wages. Before the game, they were ranked 209th, last in the world.**

SYRIA / AFC

🌐

77th (442 points)   ⇅

🚩 Syrian Football Association

✳ 1936

👤 Mosab Balhous (81)

🔫 Raja Rafe (32)

👤 Yes

🚌 Jako

🗒 **Biggest Win**
Syria 12–0 Philippines
(30 April 2001)

Biggest Defeat
Egypt 8–0 Syria
(16 October 1951)

Competitive Records 🏆

World Cup Never qualified

Asian Cup Appearances 6
Group stage 1980, 1984, 1988, 1996,
2011

Current Results

📎 **Football has not been spared by the cruel civil war. Rakka is a territory of Islamic State, who have occupied it for years. In 2016 four players from the team Al-Shabab were beheaded here for playing the 'un-Islamic' sport. Because of the hostilities Assad's national team must carry out their home games abroad. The team now train in Malaysia.**

THAILAND / AFC

THA

132nd (230 points)

Football Association of Thailand

1916

Kiatisak 'Zico' Senamuang (134)

Piyapong Piew-on (77)

Yes

Grand Sport

Biggest Win
Thailand 10–0 Brunei
(24 May 1971)

Biggest Defeat
United Kingdom (Amateur) 9–0
Thailand (26 November 1956)

Competitive Records

World Cup Never qualified

Asian Cup Appearances 7
Third place 1972

Current Results

That Thais have bony feet goes without saying. After all, they invented kickboxing. However, the national football team are not as resolute as their Muay Thai counterparts, as can be inferred from their nickname, 'chang suk' – the 'War Elephants'. Regionally, they have been making their mark, though. They have won the ASEAN championship four times and the South East Asian Cup nine times.

TAJIKISTAN / AFC

127th (255 points) ⇅

🏳 Tajikistan Football Federation

❄ 1936

👤 Fatkhullo Fatkhuloev (49)

🎯 Numonjon Hakimov (16)

👤 Yes

👟 Adidas

🧮 **Biggest Win**
Tajikistan 16–0 Guam
(26 November 2000)

Biggest Defeat
Japan 8–0 Tajikistan
(11 October 2011)

Competitive Records 🏆

World Cup Never qualified

Asian Cup Never qualified

Current Results

📎 Travel guides on Tajikistan refer to the fact that when in the Pamir region of this largely Islamic influenced country, every effort should be made to avoid telling jokes about the Aga Khan. As a precaution, the same should apply here when talking about football, even though there would be plenty of scope. Instead, we'll celebrate their outstanding 16–0 win over Guam in 2000.

TURKMENISTAN / AFC

112nd (292 points) ↕

🏳 Türkmenistanyň Futbol Federasiýasy

✳ 1992

👤 Seýitmyrat Annagulyýew (9)

🔫 Çariýar Muhadow (13)

👤 -

🚑 -

🗓 **Biggest Win**
Turkmenistan 11–0 Afghanistan
(19 November 2003)

Biggest Defeat
Tajikistan 5–0 Turkmenistan (22 June
1997); Kuwait 6–1 Turkmenistan (10
February 2000); Qatar 5–0 Turkmenistan (31 May 2004)

Competitive Records 🏆

World Cup Never qualified

Asian Cup Appearances 1
Group stage 2004

Current Results

✏

📎 **Whilst the number of smokers in Turkmenistan has noticeably dropped from 27% to 8% due to a vigorous ad campaign, the national team's star is constantly on the rise. The team reached the group stages of the Asian Cup in 2004 and managed to reach second place in the AFC Challenge Cup on two occasions. It is unlikely that smoking is the most significant contributor to these successes.**

1

2

EAST TIMOR / AFC

196th (32 points)

⚑ Federação Futebol Timor-Leste

✳ 2002

👤 Anggisu Barbosa (27)

🔫 Murilo de Almeida (6)

👤 -

🚚 -

📅 **Biggest Win**
Cambodia 1–5 East Timor
(5 October 2012)

Biggest Defeat
Malaysia 11–0 East Timor
(2 December 2009)

🏆 **Competitive Records**

World Cup Never qualified

Asian Cup Never qualified

Current Results

📎 When a team is having a rough time, those responsible tend to come up with some crazy ideas. It was decided in East Timor to grant over a dozen Brazilians citizenship of their newly founded country. This was an action that neither the fans nor the other associations were all too happy about. After some hefty wins, they eventually decided to drop their foreign-born contingent and now they are pretty average again and lose most of the time.

CHINESE TAIPEI / AFC

135th (221 points) ⇅

🏳 Chinese Taipei Football Association

✳ 1924

👤 Chen Po-liang (63)

⚽ Chen Po-liang (22)

👤 Yes

🚌 -

🗓 **Biggest Win**
Taiwan 10–0 Guam
(17 June 2007)

Biggest Defeat
Kuwait 10–0 Taiwan (9 November 2006)

Competitive Records 🏆

World Cup Never qualified

Asian Cup Appearances 2
Third place 1960

Current Results

More often than not, when there is a change of national team coach or manager, the headlines are written, but here changes to the name of the team and the country itself have been making the news. The Chinese Taipei Football Association joined the world association in 1954 as 'Taiwan', then became 'Republic of China', before finally renaming itself 'Chinese Taipei' under pressure from China. As to 'Formosa', well, let's not even go there.

UNITED ARAB EMIRATES / AFC

إتحاد الإمارات العربية المتحدة لكرة القدم
UAE FOOTBALL ASSOCIATION

73rd (474 points) ⇅

🏳 United Arab Emirates Football Association

❋ 1971
. . . .
👤 Adnan at-Talyani (164)
. . . .
⚽ Adnan at-Talyani (53)
. . . .
👤 Yes
. . . .
🚐 Adidas
. . . .

Biggest Win
Brunei 0–12 United Arab Emirates
(14 April 2001)

Biggest Defeat
United Arab Emirates 0–8 Brazil
(12 November 2005)

Competitive Records 🏆

World Cup Appearances 1
Group stage 1990

Asian Cup Appearances 10
Runners-up 1996
. . . .
Current Results

📎 **Watching football without beer? For many fans in the western world this is unimaginable. In the United Arab Emirates, alcohol is only available in tourist hotspots; locals have to be content with tea or coffee. There is also little to celebrate here, at the UAE's only World Cup finals appearance ended in elimination after three defeats.**

UZBEKISTAN / AFC

80th (437 points)

⚑ O'zbekiston Futbol Federatsiyasi

❄ 1946

👤 Server Djeparov (121)

⚽ Maksim Shatskix (34)

👤 Yes

🚌 Joma

🗓 **Biggest Win**
Uzbekistan 15–0 Mongolia
(5 December 1998)

Biggest Defeat
Japan 8–1 Uzbekistan
(17 October 2000)

Competitive Records 🏆

World Cup Never qualified

Asian Cup Appearances 7
Fourth place 2011

Current Results

📎 **For venerable international players and coaches looking to increase their pension by a few million Uzbekistani so'ms, the Uzbek League is a great place to do it. The locals have clearly learnt a lot from the likes of Eto'o, Zico, Rivaldo and Scolari, as they now rank among the strongest teams in Central Asia. In 2011, the national team finished fourth in the Asian Cup.**

1

2

VIETNAM / AFC

125th (265 points) ⇅

🏳 **Vietnam Football Federation**

❄ 1962

👤 Lê Công Vinh (83)

🔫 Lê Công Vinh (51)

👤 Yes

👕 Grand Sport

▦ **Biggest Win**
Vietnam 11–0 Guam
(23 January 2000)

Biggest Defeat
Zimbabwe 6–0 Vietnam (26 February 1997); Oman 6–0 Vietnam
(29 September 2003)

Competitive Records 🏆

World Cup Never qualified

Asian Cup Appearances 1
Quarter-finals 2007

Current Results

Until just before the end of the Vietnam War, South Vietnam's national team was trying to qualify for the 1974 World Cup. The team did not perform well. Communist countries seem to be less interested in football than capitalist ones. Perhaps their victory in the ASEAN Championship 2008 could spark a turnaround.

YEMEN / AFC

121st (268 points) ⇅

🏳 Yemen Football Association

✳ 1962

👤 Alaa Al-Sasi (33)

🥅 Ali Al-Nono (29)

👤 -

👟 Adidas

🗒 **Biggest Win**
Yemen 11–2 Bhutan
(18 February 2000)

Biggest Defeat
Libya 16–1 North Yemen
(August or September 1965)

Competitive Records 🏆

World Cup Never qualified

Asian Cup Never qualified

Current Results

🖉

📎 **A country ravaged by war, Yemen has other worries away from the world of football. The simple fact that 27 million people, or roughly 70% of the population, urgently rely on humanitarian aid, says it is probably inappropriate to mention football at this point. So, I shall use this space to appeal for a donation: please give generously to UNICEF, Medicins sans Frontiers and other organisations that support Yemen.**

The reason for the Confederation of African Football not being established until 1957 is quite simple. In the years when the European and Asian confederations were founded, there were actually only five sovereign states in the whole of Africa. It was only once the colonial powers ceded more and more independence to countries in Africa that the number of member nations increased exponentially to the point where CAF was finally set up. Today, it has 55 country member associations, which are divided into 5 different regional zones. Their most significant tournament is the Africa Cup of Nations.

ALGERIA / CAF

64th (537 points)

🏳 Fédération Algérienne de Football

❄ 1962	**Competitive Records** 🏆
👤 Lakhdar Belloumi (100)	**World Cup** Appearances 4
	Round of 16 2014
🔫 Abdelhafid Tasfaout (34)	
	Africa Cup Appearances 17
👤 Yes	Champions 1990
🚚 Adidas	**Current Results**

Biggest Win
Algeria 15–1 South Yemen
(17 August 1973)

Biggest Defeat
Hungary 9–2 Algeria
(16 August 1967)

The World Cup of 1982 saw the high point in the rather brief career of this national team. They began life after Algeria's independence in 1962. In the group stages of the 1982 World Cup in Spain, Algeria beat both West Germany and Chile and would have proceeded to the next round, were it not for the 'Disgrace of Gijon', in which the Germans and Austrians, having agreed upon a 'non-attack pact', colluded to a narrow German win, which saw both European teams advance and hang the North Africans out to dry. Not many national teams can boast a Nobel Prize-winning goalkeeper. Unfortunately, neither can Algeria. Their promising young under-18, Albert Camus, was struck down by tuberculosis before he could don the stopper's jersey for the national side.

ANGOLA / CAF

141st (201 points) ⇅

🏳 Federação Angolana de Futebol

✳ 1979

👤 Flávio Amado (91)

💥 Fabrice Akwa (37)

👤 -

👟 Adidas

📅 **Biggest Win**
Angola 7–1 Swaziland
(23 April 2000)

Biggest Defeat
Portugal 6–0 Angola
(23 March 1989)

Competitive Records

World Cup Appearances 1
Group stage 2006

Africa Cup Appearances 7
Quarter-finals 1998, 2010

Current Results

Sometimes in sport, old scores have to be settled and that is what transpired when Angola's 'Sable Antelopes' faced off against their former colonial masters, Portugal, in 2001. Emotions ran so high in this inaptly named 'friendly' that four Angolan players were shown red cards and once a fifth came off injured, the game was abandoned with Angola 5–1 down.

1

2

BURUNDI / CAF

138th (216 points) ⇵

🏴 Fédération de Football du Burundi

✳ 1948

👤 Selemani Ndikumana (48)

🔫 Selemani Ndikumana (13)

👤 -

🚗 Adidas

Biggest Win
Burundi 7–0 Djibouti
(11 March 2017)

Biggest Defeat
Congo 8–0 Burundi
(24 December 1977)

Competitive Records 🏆

World Cup Never qualified

Africa Cup Never qualified

Current Results

📎 Their first appearance in any form of international competition was a success. Burundi beat Ghana in a World Cup qualifier by 1–0 in a 1992 home fixture. This was no ordinary opponent. Ghana had just won a bronze medal at the Barcelona Olympic Games. However, Burundi has been waiting in vain for similar success ever since.

BENIN / CAF

FEDERATION BENINOISE
DE FOOTBALL

82nd (427 points) ↑↓

🏳 Fédération Béninoise de Football

✳ 1962

👤 Stéphane Sessègnon (65)

⚽ Razak Omotoyossi (21)

👤 -

👟 Airness

🧮 **Biggest Win**
Dahomey 7–0 Mauritania
(26 December 1961)

Biggest Defeat
Nigeria 10–1 Dahomey
(28 November 1959)

🏆 **Competitive Records**

World Cup Never qualified

Africa Cup Appearances 3
Group stage 2004, 2008, 2010

Current Results

📎 **When most footballing nations have a poor run of results, it is the coach who gets the chop. Well, in Benin they have a complete clear-out. The whole team were disbanded following their premature departure from the Africa Cup of Nations 2010 preliminaries. They were allowed back in just half a year later but, like before, they failed in those qualifiers too.**

BURKINA FASO / CAF

🌐

44th (705 points)   ⇅

🚩 Fédération Burkinabè de Football

❋ 1960
....

👤 Charles Kaboré (85)
....

🏹 Moumouni Dagano (34)
....

👤 Yes
....

👕 Kappa
....

🗓 **Biggest Win**
Burkina Faso 4–0 Niger (23 March
2013); Burkina Faso 5–1 Swaziland
(10 January 2015)

Biggest Defeat
Upper Volta 0–7 Algeria
(30 August 1981)

Competitive Records 🏆

World Cup Never qualified

Africa Cup Appearances 11
Runners-up 2013
....
Current Results

✎

📎 **The 'Stallions', as they are known, enjoyed their moment of glory
when they galloped into the final of the Africa Cup of Nations held in
South Africa in 2014. They lost 1–0 in that game, by a nose so to speak,
against the 'Super Eagles' of Nigeria.**

BOTSWANA / CAF

150th (176 points) ⇅

🏳 Botswana Football Association

❋ 1970

👤 Mompati Thuma (84)

⚽ Jerome Ramatlhakwane (22)

👤 Yes

🚗 -

🗓 **Biggest Win**
Botswana 6–2 Swaziland
(2 March 2002)

Biggest Defeat
Botswana 0–7 Zimbabwe
(26 August 1990)

Competitive Records 🏆

World Cup Never qualified

Africa Cup Appearances 1
Group stage 2012

Current Results

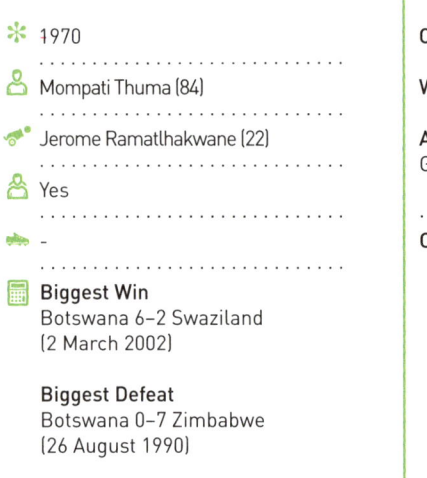

📎 **Naming the national team after an endangered species that is hunted for its skin may not be the best of omens. The 'Zebras' of Botswana could write a book on the subject after being torn to shreds by Guinea in 2012. This was the first match in 40 years of Africa Cup of Nations football in which five goals separated the two teams.**

REPUBLIC OF THE CONGO / CAF

96th (362 points) ⇅

⚑ **Fédération Congolaise de Football**

✳ 1919
....

👤 Delvin N'Dinga (50)
....

⚽ Thievy Bifouma (11)
....

👤 -
....

🚚 Adidas
....

🧮 **Biggest Win**
Republic of the Congo 11–0 São Tomé
and Príncipe (7 July 1976)

Biggest Defeat
Madagascar 8–1 Republic of the
Congo (19 April 1960)

Competitive Records 🏆

World Cup Never qualified

Africa Cup Appearances 7
Champions 1972
....
Current Results

✎

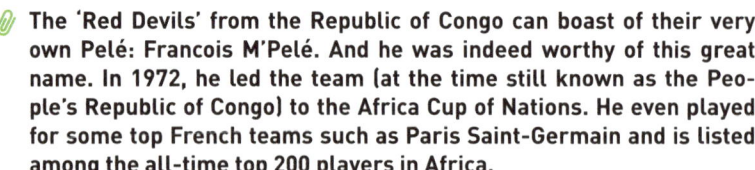

📎 The 'Red Devils' from the Republic of Congo can boast of their very
own Pelé: Francois M'Pelé. And he was indeed worthy of this great
name. In 1972, he led the team (at the time still known as the People's Republic of Congo) to the Africa Cup of Nations. He even played
for some top French teams such as Paris Saint-Germain and is listed
among the all-time top 200 players in Africa.

134

CHAD / CAF

169th (110 points)

🏳 Fédération Tchadienne de Football Association

✳ 1962

👤 Japhet N'Doram, Nabatingue Toko

🎯 -

👤 -

🚗 Adidas

🧮 **Biggest Win**
Chad 5–0 São Tomé and Príncipe
(29 June 1976)

Biggest Defeat
Congo 11–0 Chad
(28 March 1964)

🏆 Competitive Records

World Cup Never qualified

Africa Cup Never qualified

Current Results

📎 **Child mortality rate is 20%, life expectancy is 51 and the medical health care system is catastrophic. Added to that, civil war and Boko Haram terror have left the country devastated. So disbelief and anger in the wake of Chad sponsoring France's Ligue 1 is fully understandable. Hardly anyone talks about the national team.**

IVORY COAST / CAF

61st (557 points) ⇅

🏳 Fédération Ivoirienne de Football

✳ 1960

👤 Didier Zokora (123)

🔫 Didier Drogba (65)

👤 Yes

🚚 Puma

📅 **Biggest Win**
Ivory Coast 11–0 Central African
Republic (27 December 1961)

Biggest Defeat
Netherlands 5–0 Ivory Coast
(4 June 2017)

Competitive Records 🏆

World Cup Appearances 3
Group stage 2006, 2010, 2014

Africa Cup Appearances 22
Champions 1992, 2015

Current Results

📎 **Seventy-seven different languages and dialects are spoken in the home of the two-time African champions and that is in addition to the official language – French. No matter what language the Ivorian in question speaks, however, they will know two words for sure: Didier and Drogba, which are the same in all 77 tongues. Not only did this exceptional player make history at Chelsea, he is also the all-time top goal scorer for the Ivorian national team, having netted twice as many as his nearest rival.**

CAMEROON / CAF

45th (696 points)

🏳 Fédération Camerounaise de Football

✳ 1959

👤 Rigobert Song (137)

🔫 Samuel Eto'o (56)

👤 Yes

👟 Puma

🧮 **Biggest Win**
Cameroon 9–0 Chad
(April 1965)

Biggest Defeat
Russia 6–1 Cameroon (28 June 1994);
Costa Rica 5–0 Cameroon (9 March 1997)

Competitive Records 🏆

World Cup Appearances 7
Quarter-finals 1990

Africa Cup Appearances 18
Champions 1984, 1988, 2000, 2002, 2017

Current Results

📎 **No other great than Goethe is said to have popularised football in this former German colony. The Goethe in question is, however, not the prominent giant of German literature, but a photographer sharing the same name from Sierra Leone. In so doing, he kicked off a success story that saw Cameroon win the Africa Cup of Nations five times and become the first African team to reach the quarter-finals of a World Cup.**

DR CONGO / CAF

36th (764 points)

🏳 **Fédération Congolaise de Football-Association**

❄ 1962

👤 Issama Mpeko (56)

🔫 Pierre Ndaye Mulamba (32)

👤 Yes

👕 O'Neills

🖩 **Biggest Win**
DR Congo 10–1 Zambia
(22 November 1969)

Biggest Defeat
Yugoslavia 9–0 Zaire
(18 June 1974)

🏆 **Competitive Records**

World Cup Appearances 1
First group stage 1974

Africa Cup Appearances 15
Champions 1968, 1974

Current Results

📎 **Sport has often been used as a political tool by many a dictator, mainly to divert attention from their own crimes. That is how Congo, still under the name Zaire, became the venue for the famous 'Rumble in the Jungle' between George Foreman and Muhammad Ali in 1974. Football enjoyed its heyday under the dictator, Mobutu, too – Zaire won the Africa Cup of Nations twice and, in the same year that the world's top two heavyweight boxers visited the Congo, the national team became the first sub-Saharan African country to qualify for the World Cup. Whilst that side will always be remembered for Ilunga's bizarre antics kicking the ball away at a Brazilian free-kick, what was interpreted at the time as a hilarious, amateurish act was actually a political protest aimed at highlighting Mobutu's kleptocracy.**

COMOROS / CAF

130th (235 points) ↑↓

🏳 Fédération Comorienne de Football

❄ 1979

👤 Kassim Abdallah (20)

⚽ Kassim Abdallah (7)

👤 -

🚌 -

🧮 **Biggest Win**
Djibouti 2–4 Comoros
(17 December 2006)

Biggest Defeat
Mauritius 5–0 Comoros
(4 September 2003)

Competitive Records 🏆

World Cup Never qualified

Africa Cup Never qualified

Current Results

The gross domestic product of this island state in the Indian Ocean would not have been enough to cover the 222 million euro fee Paris St. Germain paid for Neymar. Even if the gifted Brazilian were to adopt Comorian citizenship, it is unlikely he would be in a position to pull any rabbits out of the hat with this outfit. However, if Comoros performances are to be judged in the light of the population and economy, then wins over teams like Djibouti are pretty impressive.

CAPE VERDE / CAF

68th (530 points) ↑↓

🏳 Federação Caboverdiana de Futebol

✳ 1982

👤 Babanco (50)

🔫 Héldon Ramos (15)

👤 -

👟 Airness

🧮 **Biggest Win**
Cape Verde 7–1 São Tomé
and Príncipe (13 June 2015)

Biggest Defeat
Guinea 4–0 Cape Verde
(9 September 2007)

Competitive Records 🏆

World Cup Never qualified

Africa Cup Appearances 2
Quarter-finals 2013

Current Results

The national side won the Amílcar Cabral Cup in their own backyard in 2000, making them champions of West Africa. The professionalism of the domestic football association, only founded after independence from Portugal, and the successful diaspora have pushed them from 182nd to 41st in the world in just a few years. They have been knocking on the door of the world's top 20 ever since. Portuguese leagues like to recruit professionals from the island and many of Cape Verdean origin, such as Nani, Patrick Vieira and Henrik Larsson, have made it big on the international stage.

CENTRAL AFRICAN REPUBLIC / CAF

🌐

123rd (266 points) ⇅

🏳 Fédération Centrafricaine de Football

✳ 1961

....

👤 Foxi Kéthévoama (32)

....

⚽ Hilaire Momi (6)

....

👤 -

....

👟 Adidas

....

📅 **Biggest Win**
Central African Republic 3–0 São Tomé and Príncipe (13 November 1999); Central African Republic 3–0 Equatorial Guinea (13 December 2009)

Biggest Defeat
Ivory Coast 11–0 Central African Republic (27 December 1961)

Competitive Records 🏆

World Cup Never qualified

Africa Cup Never qualified

....

Current Results

✏

📎 **Terrible conditions prevail in this country, one of world's poorest. The country is largely controlled by armed groups. There is not much room for football. In their first international match outside of Africa in 2011, the Central African Republic, also known as the 'Low Ubangui Fawns', were defeated 2–1 by Malta.**

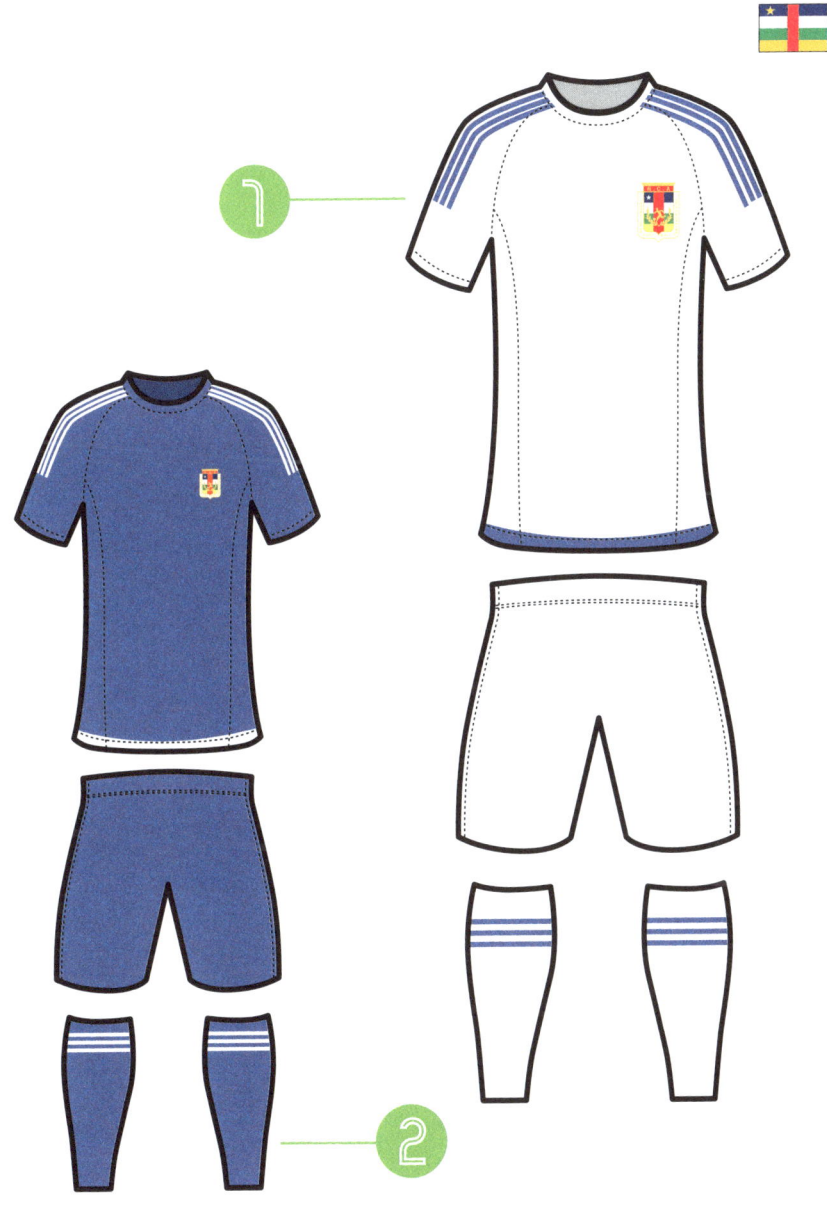

DJIBOUTI / CAF

183rd (64 points) ⇅

⚑ Fédération Djiboutienne de Football

❋ 1979

👤 Ahmed Daher (14)

🏹 Ahmed Daher (4)

👤 -

🚚 AMS Clothing

📅 **Biggest Win**
Djibouti 4–1 South Yemen
(26 February 1988)

Biggest Defeat
Djibouti 0–9 Rwanda
(13 December 2007)

🏆 Competitive Records

World Cup Never qualified

Africa Cup Never qualified

Current Results

📎 The social situation of this contrastingly desert landscaped country is more than gloomy. Unemployment stands at 60% and, according to the index of human development, the former French colony ranks 177th out of 188. The national team endure a similar fate. In their first ever attempt at qualifying for the World Cup, they finished last in their group with a goal difference of 2 scored to 30 conceded.

EGYPT / CAF

31st (805 points)

🏳 Egyptian Football Association

* 1921
....
👤 Ahmed Hassan (184)
....
🔫 Hossam Hassan (69)
....
👤 Yes
....
👟 Adidas
....
🧮 **Biggest Win**
Laos 0–15 Egypt
(15 November 1963)

Biggest Defeat
Egypt 3–11 Italy
(10 June 1928)

Competitive Records 🏆

World Cup Appearances 3
Round 1 / group stage 1934, 1990
Round of 16 1934
Qualified for 2018*

Africa Cup Appearances 23
Champions 1957, 1959, 1986, 1998,
2006, 2008, 2010
....
Current Results

📎 **Egypt is the Brazil of Africa. Well, almost. By the same token, the country, through which runs the Nile, has won the Africa Cup of Nations a record-breaking seven times. In 1934, they were the first African country to take part in the World Cup. Egyptian football has been overshadowed by the riots in the stadium at Port Said in 2012, when 74 people were killed and nearly a thousand injured. But, in 2018, Egypt partake in their first World Cup since Italia 90.**

* Kit as far as known 3 January 2018

EQUATORIAL GUINEA / CAF

145th (187 points)

Federación Ecuatoguineana de Fútbol

* 1960

Randy (34)

Emilio Nsue (5)

Yes

Hummel

Biggest Win
Equatorial Guinea 4–0 South Sudan
(4 September 2016)

Biggest Defeat
Congo 6–0 Equatorial Guinea
(13 December 1990)

Competitive Records

World Cup Never qualified

Africa Cup Appearances 2
Fourth place 2015

Current Results

The only way for the more mediocre teams of the world to reach the final of a big championship is to be the host nation. In 2012 and together with Gabon, Equatorial Guinea were co-hosts of the Africa Cup of Nations and reached the quarter-final stage. Notably, there was a Spanish look to the side's line-up: Spanish is one of the country's official languages and many descendants of former refugees from the Franco era live there.

1

2

ERITREA / CAF

206th (0 points) ↑↓

Eritrean National Football Federation

* 1992

👤 Sirak Beyene (5)

Henok Goitom (1)

👤 -

🚚 AMS Clothing

📅 **Biggest Win**
Eritrea 3–1 Somalia
(5 December 2009)

Biggest Defeat
Ghana 5–0 Eritrea (28 February 1999);
Angola 6–1 Eritrea (25 March 2007)

Competitive Records 🏆

World Cup Never qualified

Africa Cup Never qualified

Current Results

📎 **A first glance at the Eritrean national team's results would make it difficult to see any positives. In all fairness, the national team have only been playing internationally since 1992. So it would be equally fair to label their unsung exits from the World Cup and the Africa Cup of Nations qualifiers as mere teething problems.**

1

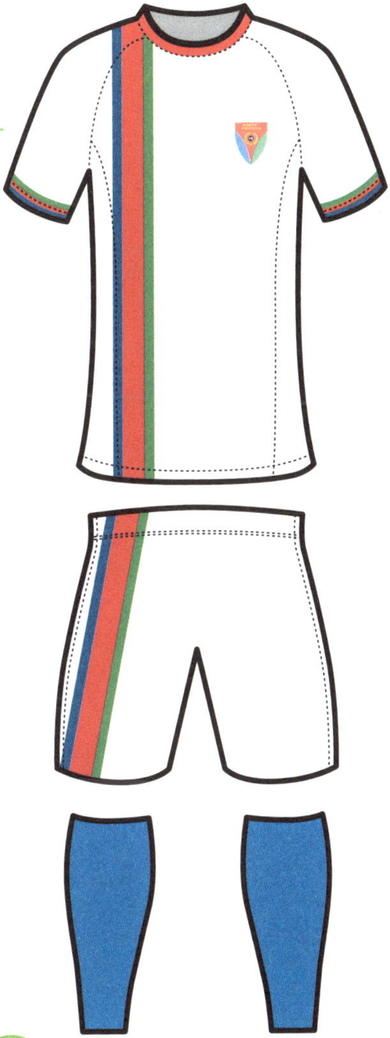

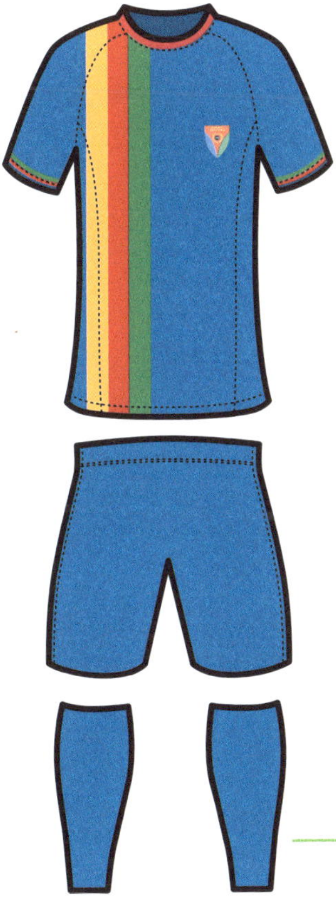

2

ETHIOPIA / CAF

145th (187 points) ⇅

🏳 **Ethiopian Football Federation**

✳ 1943

👤 Degu Debebe (51)

⚽ Getaneh Kebede (16)

👤 Yes

🚌 -

📅 **Biggest Win**
Ethiopia 8–1 Djibouti
(27 March 1983)

Biggest Defeat
Iraq 13–0 Ethiopia
(18 August 1992)

Competitive Records 🏆

World Cup Never qualified

Africa Cup Appearances 10
Champions 1962

Current Results

Even though the 'Walyas' or 'Ibex' are considered east Africa's best team, they have not made any great impression on the international stage. There are caprine comparisons here with German side FC Köln. The unfancied 'Billy Goats' of Cologne won their first Bundesliga title in 1962, the same year the 'Ibex' become champions in Africa. Me-eh! Me-eh!

GABON / CAF

93rd (370 points) ⇅

🏳 **Fédération Gabonaise de Football**

✳ 1962

👤 Didier Ovono (101)

⚽ Nguéma (23), Aubameyang (23)

👤 -

🚐 Adidas

🗓 **Biggest Win**
Gabon 7–0 Benin
(2 April 1995)

Biggest Defeat
Cameroon 6–0 Gabon (26 December 1961); Morocco 6–0 Gabon (15 November 2006)

Competitive Records 🏆

World Cup Never qualified

Africa Cup Appearances 7
Quarter-finals 1996, 2012

Current Results

📎 Gabon played in the Africa Cup of Nations quarter-final stage on two occasions and they flopped twice. Both times on penalties. Gabon has Pierre-Emerick Aubameyang, one of the best strikers in the rankings. He has scored more goals in a single Bundesliga season for Borussia Dortmund than he has managed in his eight-year career playing for his homeland.

GAMBIA / CAF

163rd (120 points)

Gambia Football Association

* 1952

👤 Ebou Sillah (110)

🔫 Alagie Biri Njie (30)

👤 -

👕 Adidas

🗓 **Biggest Win**
Gambia 6–0 Lesotho
(12 October 2002)

Biggest Defeat
Guinea 8–0 Gambia
(14 May 1972)

Competitive Records

World Cup Never qualified

Africa Cup Never qualified

Current Results

 Bad passes are always frustrating, but they have probably never been as momentous as what happened to Gambia in May 2014. The senior team and all its junior teams were banned from all continental competitions for two years by the African Federation, because five of the under-20s players were caught using forged passports.

GHANA / CAF

51st (657 points)

🏴 Ghana Football Association

❄ 1957

👤 Asamoah Gyan (106)

🎯 Asamoah Gyan (51)

👤 Yes

👟 Puma

📅 **Biggest Win**
Kenya 0–13 Ghana
(12 December 1965)

Biggest Defeat
Bulgaria 10–0 Ghana
(14 October 1968)

Competitive Records

World Cup Appearances 3
Quarter-finals 2010

Africa Cup Appearances 21
Champions 1963, 1965, 1978, 1982

Current Results

📎 **It took a major footballing force like Brazil to bring Ghana's 'Black Stars' to a halt in the World Cup 2006 knock-out rounds. On the other hand, Ghana's youth teams the 'Black Starlets', 'Black Satellites' and 'Black Meteors' have already proved their worth by winning multiple world titles.**

GUINEA-BISSAU / CAF

88th (403 points) ⇅

🏳 Federação de Futebol da Guiné-Bissau

✳ 1974

👤 Zezinho (25)

🔫 Cicero (6)

👤 -

🚌 Qelemes

📋 **Biggest Win**
Benin 2–7 Guinea-Bissau
(3 November 2001)

Biggest Defeat
Guinea 7–0 Guinea-Bissau
(22 July 2017)

Competitive Records 🏆

World Cup Never qualified

Africa Cup Appearances 1
Group stage 2017

Current Results

📎 **Located on Africa's west coast, Guinea-Bissau enjoyed their greatest footballing success when coming second at the Amilcar Cabral Cup in 1983. This tournament involving West African teams was held between 1979 and 2007 and was in remembrance of the eponymous poet and independence campaigner. Cabral was assassinated in his homeland, the Cape Verde Islands, in 1973.**

GUINEA / CAF

66th (532 points)

Fédération Guinéenne de Football

* 1960

Pascal Feindouno (90)

Pascal Feindouno (29)

Yes

Airness

Biggest Win
Guinea 14–0 Mauritania
(20 May 1972)

Biggest Defeat
Zaire 6–0 Guinea
(2 July 1972)

Competitive Records

World Cup Never qualified

Africa Cup Appearances 11
Runners-up 1976

Current Results

Many players from this West African country are a sensation abroad.
In the English Premier League, the Championship and the Bundesliga,
players like Titi Camara, Kaba Diawara, Pablo Thiam and Naby Keita
are causing spotlights to be shone on Guinean football.

KENYA / CAF

111st (300 points)

🏳 Football Kenya Federation

❇ 2012 (1960)

👤 Mike Origi (120)

⚽ Dennis Oliech (34)

👤 Yes

🚌 Joma

🗒 **Biggest Win**
Kenya 9–1 Djibouti
(15 August 1998)

Biggest Defeat
Kenya 0–13 Ghana
(12 December 1965)

Competitive Records 🏆

World Cup Never qualified

Africa Cup Never qualified

Current Results

The team is also known as 'The Harambee Stars'. The nickname is derived from a Kiswahili word roughly meaning: 'Let's pull together'. This side have hardly pulled anything off in world football, having failed to ever qualify for a single World Cup tournament. The furthest they reached was the preliminary rounds of the Africa Cup of Nations, although they do boast proverbial brick outhouse Victor Wanyama as their totemic captain.

1

2

LIBERIA / CAF

134th (224 points) ⇅

🏳 Liberia Football Association

❋ 1936

👤 Kelvin Sebwe (73)

🔫 James Debbah (42)

👤 -

🚌 Adidas

🖩 **Biggest Win**
Liberia 5–0 Djibouti
(29 March 2016)

Biggest Defeat
Ghana 6–0 Liberia
(6 April 1975)

Competitive Records 🏆

World Cup Never qualified

Africa Cup Appearances 2
Group stage 1996, 2002

Current Results

📎 **The national team's nickname is the 'Lone Stars', which is totally appropriate given that Liberia only really ever had one. The name? George Weah. He was actually crowned Africa's footballer of the century and enjoyed success at both Paris Saint-Germain and AC Milan. As Weah truly was the 'Lone Star', the national team are still yet to achieve any initial success.**

LIBYA / CAF

77th (442 points)

Libyan Football Federation

1962

Tarik El Taib (77)

Fawzi Al-Issawi (40)

-

Adidas

Biggest Win
Libya 21–0 Oman
(1 April 1966)

Biggest Defeat
Egypt 10–2 Libya
(29 July 1953)

Competitive Records

World Cup Never qualified

Africa Cup Appearances 3
Runners-up 1982

Current Results

Many will recall revolutionary leader Muammar al-Gaddafi's son Saadi coming on for Perugia to replace Jay Bothroyd in the last 15 minutes of a match against Juventus in 2004. Saadi's dad was best mates with Italian President Silvio Berlusconi. Funny that. The 'Green Book', in which Gaddafi communicated his wisdom to the people, seems to have contained neither wise nor useful information about football, which possibly explains why the country was only able to win its first title after the fall of the dictator in 2011. In 2014, Libya won the Africa Cup of Nations, while Saadi was being tortured in jail awaiting trial for murder.

LESOTHO / CAF

144th (188 points) ↕

⚑ Lesotho Football Association

✳ 1932

👤 Pakalitha Ngele (112)

⚽ Salemane Seeiso (23)

👤 -

🚌 -

🗓 **Biggest Win**
Lesotho 5–0 Swaziland
(14 April 2006)

Biggest Defeat
Zambia 9–0 Lesotho
(8 August 1988)

Competitive Records 🏆

World Cup Never qualified

Africa Cup Never qualified

Current Results

🖉

📎 The name of the stadium opened by Sepp Blatter in 2002 is 'Setsoto', meaning 'The Amazement'. But so far, there has been very little to be amazed about with the Lesotho national side. The national team – 'Likuena' or 'The Crocodiles' as they are known – have not quite developed a strong enough bite to damage any of their opponents in African football.

MADAGASCAR / CAF

108th (309 points) ⇅

🏳 **Fédération Malagasy de Football**

❄ 1961

👤 Paulin Voavy (29)

⚽ Faneva Andriatsima (8)

👤 -

👕 Adidas

🗓 **Biggest Win**
Madagascar 8–1 Republic of the
Congo (19 April 1960)

Biggest Defeat
Mauritius 7–0 Madagascar
(31 July 1952)

Competitive Records 🏆

World Cup Never qualified

Africa Cup Never qualified

Current Results

📎 **As a result of Madagascar deciding to withdraw from the 1996 Africa Cup of Nations qualifiers, FIFA barred them from the subsequent qualifiers in 1998. And to this day, they are still waiting for their first participation in a major tournament. That said, the Madagascans have made a very confident start in the qualifying rounds of the 2019 Africa Cup, having won four times already.**

MOROCCO / CAF

40th (738 points) ↕

⚑ Fédération Royale Marocaine de Football

✳ 1955

👤 Abdelmajid Dolmy (124)

⚽ Salaheddine Bassir (43)

👤 Yes

🚗 Adidas

🗒 **Biggest Win**
Morocco 13–1 Saudi Arabia
(6 September 1961)

Biggest Defeat
Hungary 6–0 Morocco
(11 October 1964)

Competitive Records 🏆

World Cup Appearances 5
Round of 16 1986
Qualified for 2018*

Africa Cup Appearances 16
Champions 1976

Current Results

🖉

📎 By African standards, Morocco is a rather small country. In no way, however, does that stop its team from performing well. The 1976 African champions have already taken part in four World Cup tournaments. In 1986, the Moroccans even made it to the second round. At the 1998 World Cup in France, they played fantastically well, but were sadly eliminated at the group stage.

* Kit as far as known 3 January 2018

MALI / CAF

72nd (493 points)

Fédération Malienne de Football

1960

Seydou Keïta (102)

Seydou Keïta (25)

Yes

Airness

Biggest Win
Mali 11–0 Mauritania
(1 October 1972)

Biggest Defeat
Algeria 7–0 Mali (13 November 1988);
Kuwait 8–1 Mali (5 September 1997)

Competitive Records

World Cup Never qualified

Africa Cup Appearances 10
Runners-up 1972

Current Results

The beauty of football is that things can only get better. And in Mali, there is very good reason to hope for a better future. The national team, better known as the 'Eagles', has yet to win any titles, but the junior team has really stepped up to the plate. In 2015, the under-17s won the African championship, and they subsequently became the world second best in their age group.

MOZAMBIQUE / CAF

110th (304 points)

🏳 Federação Moçambicana de Futebol

✳ 1976

👤 Dário Monteiro (85)

⚽ Tico-Tico (27)

👤 -

🚌 -

🖩 **Biggest Win**
Mozambique 6–1 Lesotho (10 August 1980); Mozambique 5–0 South Sudan (18 May 2014)

Biggest Defeat
Zimbabwe 6–0 Mozambique (20 April 1980)

Competitive Records 🏆

World Cup Never qualified

Africa Cup Appearances 4
Group stage 1986, 1996, 1998, 2010

Current Results

📎 **Not only did the Europeans uninhibitedly extract the mineral resources of their colonies, they also robbed Mozambique of its most valuable footballing jewel, Eusébio. Born in this south eastern African country, he became one of the world's greatest stars in the 1960s. At the 1966 World Cup, he was top scorer. Ironically, he was scoring for Portugal, because Mozambique was still a Portuguese colony.**

MAURITIUS / CAF

Mauritius Football Association

* 1952

Richard Joubert (80)

Andy Sophie (11)

-

Adidas

Biggest Win
Mauritius 15–2 Réunion
(date unknown, 1950)

Biggest Defeat
Seychelles 7–0 Mauritius
(19 July 2008); Senegal 7–0 Mauritius
(9 October 2010)

Competitive Records

World Cup Never qualified

Africa Cup Appearances 1
Group stage 1974

Current Results

Mauritian national team successes are a rare occurrence, similar to the famous magenta blue stamp sought after by philatelists worldwide. The team's performances, however, are not of the kind to set your pulse racing. Their biggest and, so far, only success was to actually participate in the Africa Cup finals in 1974.

MAURITANIA / CAF

99th (354 points) ⇅

🏳 Fédération de Football de la République Islamique de Mauritanie

✳ 1961

👤 Mohamed Harouna (79)

🔫 Omar Hassan (39)

👤 -

👟 Adidas

🧮 **Biggest Win**
Mauritania 8–2 Somalia
(27 December 2006)

Biggest Defeat
Guinea 14–0 Mauritania
(20 May 1972)

Competitive Records 🏆

World Cup Never qualified

Africa Cup Never qualified

Current Results

📎 **The media often speaks of a modern slave trade when referring to the transfer policy of football players. This former French colony was the last country on earth to abolish slavery in 1981. So, it was all the more shocking when an organisation called SOS Esclaves (SOS Slaves) released a statement claiming there are still 600,000 slaves in Mauritania. This is a major tragedy – hidden from the outside world, much like the Mauritanian national team.**

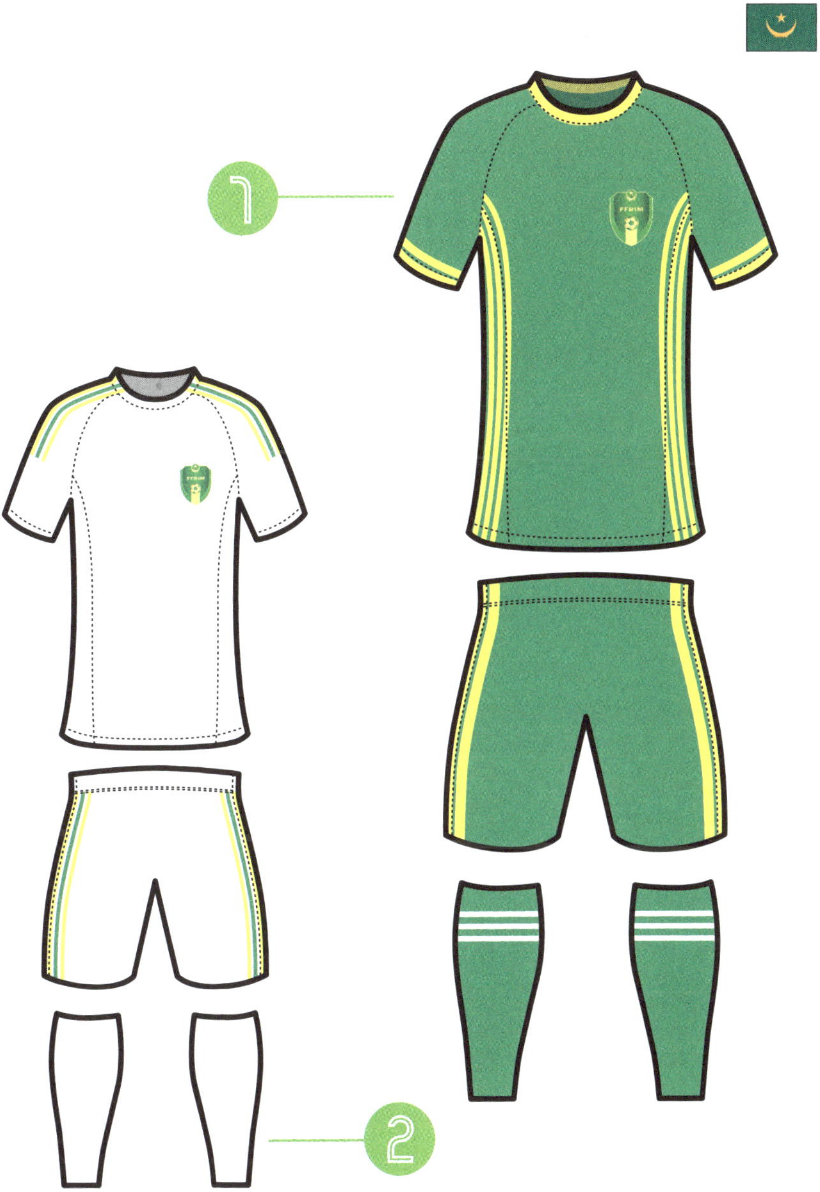

MALAWI / CAF

126th (260 points) ⇅

🏳 Football Association of Malawi

✳ 1966
....

👤 Kinnah Phiri (115)
....

⚽ Kinnah Phiri (71)

👤 -
....

👟 Umbro
....

📅 **Biggest Win**
Malawi 8–1 Botswana (13 July 1968);
Malawi 8–1 Djibouti (31 May 2008)

Biggest Defeat
Nyasaland 0–12 Ghana
(15 October 1962)

Competitive Records 🏆

World Cup Never qualified

Africa Cup Appearances 2
Group stage 1984, 2010
....
Current Results

✐

📎 **'Gule Wamkulu', the illustrious dance paying homage to the dead in Malawi, has been embraced into UNESCO's 'Oral and Intangible Heritage of Humanity' series of 90 masterpieces. On the football pitch, however, the Malawians have not been as self-assured. So far, they have only qualified twice for the group stage of the Africa Cup of Nations.**

NAMIBIA / CAF

NFA

NAM

119th (274 points)

Namibia Football Association

1990

Johannes Hindjou (69)

Rudolph Bester (13)

Yes

Puma

Biggest Win
Namibia 8–2 Benin (15 July 2000); Namibia 6–0 Botswana (25 August 1996)

Biggest Defeat
Egypt 7–1 Namibia (8 November 1996); Egypt 8–2 Namibia (13 July 2001)

Competitive Records

World Cup Never qualified

Africa Cup Appearances 2
Group stage 1998, 2008

Current Results

Anyone thinking about getting more women involved in football management should look no further than Namibia. Despite some attractive performances, the 'Brave Warriors' are usually dozens of places behind the 'Brave Gladiators', their female counterparts, in the world rankings. The ladies are in the Top 100.

NIGERIA / CAF

50th (671 points) ⇅

🏳 Nigeria Football Federation

 1945

....

👤 Vincent Enyeama (101), Joseph Yobo (101)

....

Rashidi Yekini (37)

....

👤 Yes

....

👟 Nike

....

🗓 **Biggest Win**
Nigeria 8–1 Uganda
(23 September 1991)

Biggest Defeat
Ghana 7–0 Nigeria
(1 June 1955)

🏆 **Competitive Records**

World Cup Appearances 6
Round of 16 1994, 1998, 2014
Qualified for 2018*

Africa Cup Appearances 17
Champions 1980, 1994, 2013

....

Current Results

📎 **Nigeria's national team have undergone a bit of a transformation. In the beginning, they were known as the 'Red Devils'. After not being permitted to wear their usual scarlet red jerseys in a game against Egypt in 1960, the players had to wear a green striped bib and became known as the 'Green Eagles'. Nowadays, and by virtue of numerous international successes, they are called the 'Super Eagles'.**

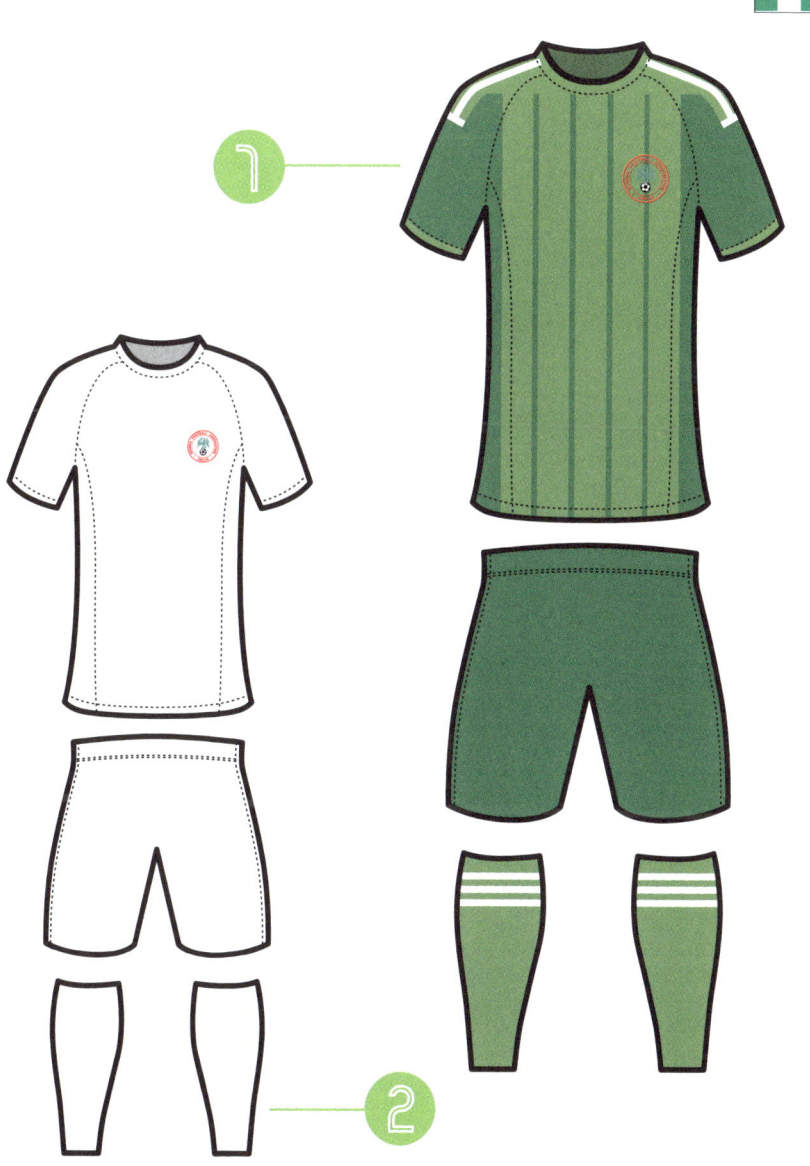

* Kit as far as known 3 January 2018

NIGER / CAF

108th (309 points) ↕

⚐ Fédération Nigérienne de Football

❋ 1967
....
👤 Kassaly Daouda (61)
....
🏹 Moussa Maâzou (45)
....
👤 -
....
🚍 -
....
📅 **Biggest Win**
Niger 7–1 Mauritania
(12 October 1990)

Biggest Defeat
Republic of the Congo 10–0 Niger
(27 December 1961)

Competitive Records 🏆

World Cup Never qualified

Africa Cup Appearances 2
Group stage 2012, 2013
....
Current Results

✎

📎 **The national team of Niger is nicknamed 'Ménas'. The word in the local Hausa language describes an endangered species: the Dama gazelle. This almost heraldic symbol, also emblazoned upon the national association's logo, does not seem to be giving the national football team much luck. Reaching the quarters of the Africa Cup of Nations is their sole success so far.**

SOUTH AFRICA / CAF

SOUTH AFRICAN FOOTBALL ASSOCIATION

81st (434 points)

South African Football Association

❄ 1936

👤 Aaron Mokoena (107)

🔫 Benni McCarthy (32)

👤 Yes

👟 Puma

📅 **Biggest Win**
Australia 0–8 South Africa
(17 September 1955)

Biggest Defeat
Brazil 5–0 South Africa
(5 March 2014)

Competitive Records 🏆

World Cup Appearances 3
Group stage 1998, 2002, 2010

Africa Cup Appearances 8
Champions 1996

Current Results

📎 **With prominent international cricket and rugby sides, South Africa came late to the soccer game, but in their first performances after the end of apartheid, they won the people's hearts. Fans baptised the young team 'Bafana, Bafana', meaning 'The Boys'. South Africa won the Africa Cup of Nations in 1996 and hosted the World Cup in 2010.**

RWANDA / CAF

120th (269 points)

Fédération Rwandaise de Football Association

1972

Haruna Niyonzima (75)

Olivier Karekezi (25)

Yes

AMS Clothing

Biggest Win
Djibouti 0–9 Rwanda
(13 December 2007)

Biggest Defeat
Tunisia 5–0 Rwanda (10 April 1983);
Uganda 5–0 Rwanda (1 August 1998)

Competitive Records

World Cup Never qualified

Africa Cup Appearances 1
Group stage 2004

Current Results

One might think that only witchcraft could help this chronically luckless national team out of its misery. Yet, witchcraft was indeed banned by the Rwanda Football Federation in 2016. Any players found guilty of it are banned for three games and their coaches get a four game suspension. It's a while ago since the unlucky Ugandan Premier League trio of Patrick 'Crespo' Asiku, Herbert Kakande and Asuman Bajampola were banned for practising witchcraft, but their banishment stands as a sobering reminder for their Rwandan counterparts to cut the hocus-pocus out of their game. There is hope in youth. Rwanda's under-17s were runners-up in the Africa Cup in 2011. Let's just hope that the young lads stick to wizardry on the wing and steer clear of the other mumbo-jumbo.

SENEGAL / CAF

23rd (884 points)

⚑ Fédération Sénégalaise de Football

❋ 1960

👤 Henri Camara (99)

🔫 Henri Camara (29)

👤 Yes

🚌 Romai

🧮 **Biggest Win**
Senegal 7–0 Mauritius
(9 October 2010)

Biggest Defeat
Czechoslovakia 11–0 Senegal
(2 November 1966)

Competitive Records 🏆

World Cup Appearances 2
Quarter-finals 2002
Qualified for 2018*

Africa Cup Appearances 14
Runners-up 2002

Current Results

📎 What a debut! At the 2002 World Cup, joint-hosted by Japan and South Korea, Senegal started with a bang. It was their first ever World Cup finals and they beat France 1–0. Two more draws followed and they were in the round of 16 before going on to beat Sweden 2–1. The Lions' dream only came to an end in the quarter-finals, when they went down 1–0 in a close game against Turkey.

1

2

* Kit as far as known 3 January 2018

SEYCHELLES / CAF

189th (51 points) ⇅

🏳 Seychelles Football Federation

✳ 1979

👤 Carl Hoprich (4)

🏹 Philip Zialor (11)

👤 -

🚌 Adidas

📅 **Biggest Win**
Seychelles 9–0 Maldives
(27 August 1979)

Biggest Defeat
Madagascar 6–0 Seychelles
(27 August 1990)

Competitive Records 🏆

World Cup Never qualified

Africa Cup Never qualified

Current Results

📎 **The marvellous beaches of the Seychelles in the Indian ocean are often used as an exotic location for TV advertisements, although they rarely advertise football here. Being in the Southern African Zone of CAF, on the few occasions that the national team does play, it is likely to be in a similar dream destination such as Mauritius, Réunion, the Maldives or Namibia, making away days something of a holiday.**

SIERRA LEONE / CAF

97th (360 points) ↕

🏳 Sierra Leone Football Association

✳ 1967

👤 Umaru Bangura (42)

⚽ Gibrila (4)

👤 -

👟 AMS Clothing

📅 **Biggest Win**
Sierra Leone 4–0 São Tomé and
Príncipe (22 April 2000)

Biggest Defeat
Mali 6–0 Sierra Leone
(17 June 2007)

Competitive Records 🏆

World Cup Never qualified

Africa Cup Appearances 2
Group stage 1994, 1996

Current Results

📎 During the suffering from the harsh consequences of years of civil war, an Ebola epidemic broke out in Sierra Leone in 2014. It is hard to build a successful team in such devastating conditions. Nevertheless, the national team, also known as the 'Leone Stars', have been able to notch up some notable successes and pushed into 50th place in the world rankings.

SOMALIA / CAF

206th (0 points) ↕

⚑ **Somali Football Federation**

❋ 1969

👤 Adam Osman

🏹 Jibril Heersare

👤 -

🚌 Adidas

🧮 **Biggest Win**
Somalia 5–2 Mauritania
(7 August 1985)

Biggest Defeat
North Korea 14–0 Somalia
(1 November 1963)

Competitive Records 🏆

World Cup Never qualified

Africa Cup Never qualified

Current Results

📎 **Even in football, the situation in the region of the Horn of Africa is dire. According to a report from the magazine *Elf Freunde*, two fans were shot dead by terrorists in 2006 for watching a game on television. In 2011, a journalist was murdered for reporting about football and, in the same year, Somalia's most promising talent, Abdi Salaan Mohamed Ali, was killed by a car bomb. Three internationals were killed by the massive truck bomb blast in Mogadishu in 2017. Amidst such tragedy, one can imagine, football is not the first thing on people's minds.**

SOUTH SUDAN / CAF

SSFA

152nd (172 points) ⇅

🏳 South Sudan Football Association

✴ 2011

👤 Jumma Ginaro (22)

⚽ James Moga (6)

👤 -

👕 AMS Clothing

📅 **Biggest Win**
South Sudan 6–0 Djibouti
(28 March 2017)

Biggest Defeat
South Sudan 0–5 Mozambique
(18 May 2014)

Competitive Records 🏆

World Cup Never qualified

Africa Cup Never qualified

Current Results

📎 This country, barely six years old, is considered a failed one, mainly because of its never-ending civil war. This did not stop FIFA, however, from taking the country on as its 209th member in 2012. The 'Bright Stars', as they are nicknamed, won their first games in 2015 with victories against Equatorial Guinea and Malawi. In Ethiopia, they even reached the quarter-finals at the East and Central African Championship.

SÃO TOMÉ AND PRÍNCIPE / CAF

177th (94 points) ↕

🏳 Federação Santomense de Futebol

🌱 1975

👤 Nai (12)

🔫 Luís Leal (3)

👤 -

🚌 Lacatoni

🧮 **Biggest Win**
São Tomé and Príncipe 2–0 Equatorial
Guinea (14 November 1999);
São Tomé and Príncipe 2–0 Sierra
Leone (8 April 2000)

Biggest Defeat
Congo 11–0 São Tomé and Príncipe
(7 July 1976)

Competitive Records 🏆

World Cup Never qualified

Africa Cup Never qualified

Current Results

🖊

📎 **They used to write 'Hic sunt leones', meaning 'Here be lions', on ancient maps of unexplored regions. Unfortunately, there is very little on these islands in the Gulf of Guinea but birds, frogs and snakes. The national team typically find themselves at the bottom of the table, despite some respectable wins over weaker local opposition.**

SUDAN / CAF

137th (219 points) ↑↓

🏳 Sudan Football Association

✳ 1968

👤 Muhannad Tahir (63)

🎯 Muhannad Tahir (14)

👤 -

👟 Adidas

🗓 **Biggest Win**
Sudan 15–0 Oman
(2 September 1965)

Biggest Defeat
South Korea 8–0 Sudan
(10 September 1979)

Competitive Records 🏆

World Cup Never qualified

Africa Cup Appearances 8
Champions 1970

Current Results

📎 **Located in the north east of Africa by the Red Sea, Sudan has a very young population. Almost 40% of its inhabitants are younger than 15 years old. Most of the Sudanese were not yet born when the country achieved its first and only success – the 'Desert Hawks' won the Africa Cup in their own country in 1970.**

SWAZILAND / CAF

133rd (225 points) ⇅

🏴 **National Football Association of Swaziland**

※ 1930

👤 Mlungisi Ngubane (91)

🔫 Sibusiso Dlamini (26)

👤 -

👟 Adidas

🖩 **Biggest Win**
Djibouti 0–6 Swaziland
(8 October 2015)

Biggest Defeat
Egypt 10–0 Swaziland
(22 March 2013)

Competitive Records 🏆

World Cup Never qualified

Africa Cup Never qualified

Current Results

📎 The old Swazi saying goes that politics is dictated by the king, the so-called 'Ngwenyana' (lion) and the king's mother, the 'Ndlovukati' (female elephant). Were they to bestow such animal titles on the football team, they would probably be the shrews or fruit bats. Up till now, the team has only played a modest role in the regional championship football competitions in southern Africa.

TANZANIA / CAF

142nd (139 points) ↕

🏳 Tanzania Football Federation

❄ 1930

👤 Mrisho Ngasa (99)

⚽ Mrisho Ngasa (24)

👤 Yes

🚍 -

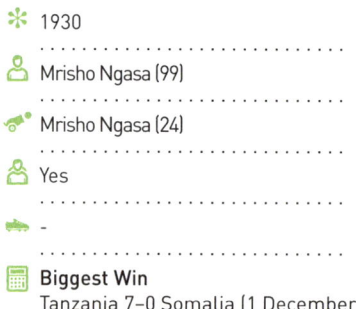

📅 **Biggest Win**
Tanzania 7–0 Somalia (1 December 1995); Tanzania 7–0 Somalia (1 December 2012)

Biggest Defeat
Ethiopia 7–0 Tanzania (8 October 1969); Algeria 7–0 Tanzania (17 October 2015)

Competitive Records 🏆

World Cup Never qualified

Africa Cup Appearances 1
Group stage 1980

Current Results

📎 **Everyone is totally football crazy in this east African country. The streets are typically awash with people sporting soccer shirts. Nicknamed the 'Taifa Stars', the national team unfortunately do not do the enthusiasm of the fans any justice at all as they have appeared just once at the Africa Cup of Nations – only to be eliminated in the first round.**

TOGO / CAF

🏳 Fédération Togolaise de Football

✳ 1954

👤 Emmanuel Adebayor (76)

➶ Emmanuel Adebayor (31)

👤 -

🚑 -

🗓 **Biggest Win**
Togo 6–0 Swaziland
(11 October 2008)

Biggest Defeat
Morocco 7–0 Togo (28 October 1979);
Tunisia 7–0 Togo (7 January 2000)

Competitive Records 🏆

World Cup Appearances 1
Group stage 2006

Africa Cup Appearances 8
Quarter-finals 2013

Current Results

🖉

📎 **Bogus national team shirts may be fairly common but a phoney national team is something of a novelty. But that is what Bahrain's national team coach discovered when his team beat Togo 3–0 in a game held at Riffa in 2010. The coach questioned the Togo players' fitness over the 90 minutes and it turned out he had been watching a team of complete unknowns. The Togolese football association told FIFA they hadn't actually sent out a team at all. It turned out that a fake agent had assembled a team of ringers and done a bunk with the takings. Togo are not really that bad a side, as their showing in the World Cup finals of 2006 proved.**

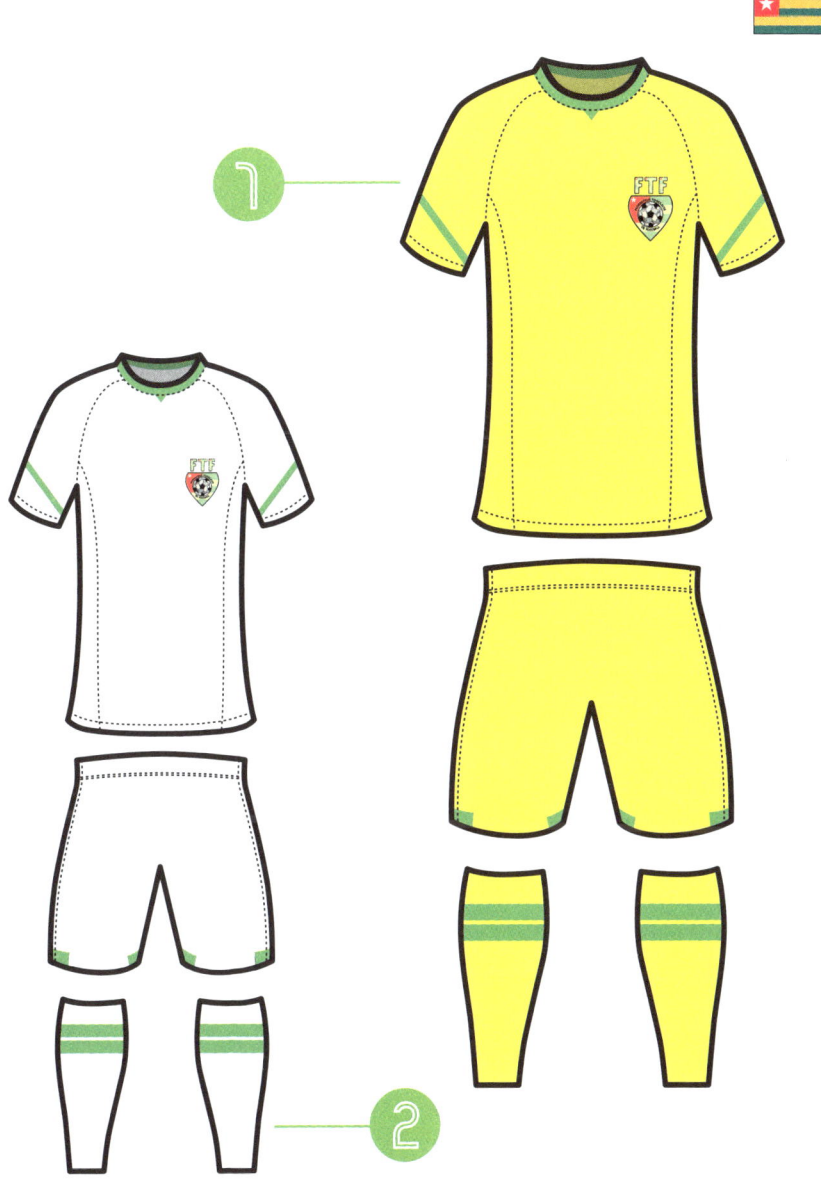

TUNISIA / CAF

27th (838 points)

🏳 Fédération Tunisienne de Football

✳ 1956

👤 Sadok Sassi (116)

⚽ Issam Jemâa (36)

👤 Yes

👟 Uhlsport

🖩 **Biggest Win**
Tunisia 7–0 Malawi (26 March 2005);
Tunisia 8–1 Djibouti (12 June 2015)

Biggest Defeat
Hungary 10–1 Tunisia
(24 July 1960)

Competitive Records

World Cup Appearances 5
(First) group stage 1978, 1998, 2002,
2006
Qualified for 2018*

Africa Cup Appearances 1
Champions 2004

Current Results

📎 **The 'Eagles of Carthage', as they are known, certainly seem to have inherited some of their ancestor Hannibal's strategic genius. After all, the team from north Africa have reached four World Cup finals and even teams such as Germany have nearly met their downfall against the 'Eagles', who have also won the Africa Cup of Nations in 2004.**

* Kit as far as known 3 January 2018

UGANDA / CAF

74th (471 points)

🏳 Federation of Uganda Football Associations

✳ 1924

👤 Simeon Masaba (87)

🎯 Geofrey Massa (21)

👤 Yes

🚑 -

📅 **Biggest Win**
Uganda 13–1 Kenya
(1932)

Biggest Defeat
Egypt 6–0 Uganda (30 July 1995);
Tunisia 6–0 Uganda (28 February 1999)

Competitive Records

World Cup Never qualified

Africa Cup Appearances 2
Runners-up 1978

Current Results

When Idi Amin told German coach Burkhard Pape of the minimum targets he expected him to achieve, there was no doubt he was slightly delusional. The 'Cranes' were to be moulded into the best soccer team in the universe by the journeyman German. After all, they did manage to win the Africa Cup and remained one of east Africa's strongest teams throughout the uncrowned King of Scotland's reign of terror. Pape's win-rate was almost 60% and he went on to manage Egypt and a number of Asian national teams.

1

2

ZAMBIA / CAF

75th (449 points) ⇅

🏳 **Football Association of Zambia**

❋ 1929

👤 Kennedy Mweene (116)

🔫 Godfrey Chitalu (79)

👤 Yes

👟 -

📅 **Biggest Win**
Zambia 9–0 Kenya (13 November 1978); Zambia 9–0 Lesotho (8 August 1988)
Biggest Defeat
Zambia 1–10 DR Congo (22 November 1969); Belgium 9–0 Zambia (3 June 1994)

Competitive Records 🏆

World Cup Never qualified

Africa Cup Appearances 16
Champions 2012

Current Results

🖊

📎 At almost the same place where a tragedy happened, so too followed a triumph. In 1993, a plane crashed shortly after refuelling in Libreville. On board were 18 Zambian internationals on their way to a World Cup qualifier. Nineteen years later in Libreville, the Zambian national team defeated Ivory Coast in the final, to win the Africa Cup of Nations.

ZIMBABWE / CAF

103rd (323 points)

🏳 Zimbabwe Football Association

✳ 1965

👤 Peter Ndlovu (100)

💥 Peter Ndlovu (38)

👤 Yes

🚌 -

🧮 **Biggest Win**
Botswana 0–7 Zimbabwe
(26 August 1990)

Biggest Defeat
Zaire 5–0 Zimbabwe
(4 June 1995)

Competitive Records 🏆

World Cup Never qualified

Africa Cup Appearances 3
Group stage 2004, 2006, 2017

Current Results

📎 At the Africa Games qualifications in 2013, the 'Warriors' experienced an ignominious defeat. After being knocked out by Angola, the entire team was banned on the basis of suspected corruption. Eighty players had been banned a year before that, meaning that all hope for future success lies with Zimbabwe's youth teams.

CONCACAF

CONCACAF

The Confederation of North, Central America and Caribbean Association Football was set up in 1961 and unified the national associations of each geographic region. Of the 41 national associations, the majority of these come from the Caribbean Football Union. The confederation's biggest competition in the CONCACAF Gold Cup.

ANGUILLA / CONCACAF

206th (0 points) ⇅

⚑ Anguilla Football Association

✳ 1990

👤 Girdon Connor (19)

🎯 Richard O'Connor (5)

👤 -

🚌 -

🖩 **Biggest Win**
Anguilla 4–1 Montserrat
(8 February 2001)

Biggest Defeat
Guyana 14–0 Anguilla
(19 April 1998)

🏆 **Competitive Records**

World Cup Never qualified

Gold Cup Never qualified

Current Results

 It sounds puzzling, but there seems to be an everlasting storm cloud over the Leeward Islands. The 0–0 away draw against the Dominican Republic is seen as the greatest success of the national team. On the plus side, however, there has been the odd consolation goal or two and even a 4–1 walk-in-the-park victory over Montserrat, one of the weakest teams in world soccer.

179th (92 points) ⇅

🚩 **Arubaanse Voetbal Bond**

✳ 1932

👤 Theric Ruiz

⚽ -

👤 -

🚌 Admiral

📋 **Biggest Win**
Aruba 7–0 British Virgin Islands
(1 June 2014)

Biggest Defeat
Trinidad and Tobago 11–0 Aruba
(4 June 1989)

Competitive Records 🏆

World Cup Never qualified

Gold Cup Never qualified

Current Results

📎 **This Caribbean island belongs to Holland, but is light years away from its colonial fatherland in football terms. The team's greatest achievement was to reach the third round of the qualifying competition for the 2018 World Cup. They had a little help on the way. They had lost twice to Barbados only to discover that Barbados had fielded a player who was already on a yellow card ban. This led to Aruba going into the next round by default, in which they promptly lost to St. Vincent and the Grenadines.**

ANTIGUA AND BARBUDA / CONCACAF

140th (209 points) ⇅

🏳 Antigua and Barbuda Football Association

❄ 1928

👤 Peter Byers (79)

🔫 Peter Byers (39)

👤 -

🚂 Admiral

🗒 **Biggest Win**
Antigua and Barbuda 10–0 US Virgin Islands (11 October 2011)

Biggest Defeat
Trinidad and Tobago 11–1 Antigua and Barbuda (10 November 1972)

Competitive Records 🏆

World Cup Never qualified

Gold Cup Never qualified

Current Results

📎 **No other head of state rules over more national teams than Queen Elizabeth II. Antigua and Barbuda is one of them and it is by no means the worst side. In the Caribbean Cup of 1998, they came a respectable fourth. One memorable game came when Antigua and Barbuda led twice against Cuba only to suffer a 4–3 defeat at the final whistle.**

BAHAMAS / CONCACAF

206th (0 points) ⇅

⚑ Bahamas Football Association

✳ 1967

👤 Lesly St. Fleur (12), Cameron Hepple (12)

🔫 Lesly St. Fleur (6)

👤 -

🚑 -

📅 **Biggest Win**
Bahamas 6–0 Turks and Caicos
Islands (9 July 2011)

Biggest Defeat
Mexico 13–0 Bahamas
(28 April 1987)

Competitive Records 🏆

World Cup Never qualified

Gold Cup Never qualified

Current Results

✏

📎 **Palms gently rustle in the tropical breeze; the turquoise ocean kisses the snow white beach. Who does not think about a relaxing holiday when they think about the Bahamas? It is exactly the same for the football players of this paradisiacal island state. What other excuse could they have for pulling out of big tournaments at the last minute?**

BERMUDA / CONCACAF

180th (72 points)

🏳 Bermuda Football Association

※ 1928

👤 Damon Ming (42)

🔫 Shaun Goater (32)

👤 -

🔫 -

📅 **Biggest Win**
Bermuda 13–0 Montserrat
(29 February 2004)

Biggest Defeat
Canada 6–0 Bermuda (8 May 1983);
Mexico 6–0 Bermuda (17 May 1987)

Competitive Records

World Cup Never qualified

Gold Cup Never qualified

Current Results

What springs to mind when thinking about Bermuda – knee-length shorts and the mysterious triangle, perhaps? One of Britain's first black footballers, Clyde Cyril Best MBE, had to put up with a lot of that after he vanished from the coral islands in 1968 and headed to England. In his West Ham shorts, the robust centre forward made 174 appearances and netted 47 goals. In contrast to the numerous ships and aeroplanes, Clyde did not disappear, but resurfaced to become the national coach of Bermuda in 1997.

BELIZE / CONCACAF

157th (135 points)

🏳 Football Federation of Belize

❋ 1980

👤 Elroy Smith (44)

🔫 Deon McCaulay (21)

👤 -

👟 Nike

🗓 **Biggest Win**
Belize 7–1 Nicaragua
(17 April 2002)

Biggest Defeat
Costa Rica 7–0 Belize (17 March
1999); Mexico 7–0 Belize (21 June
2008)

Competitive Records 🏆

World Cup Never qualified

Gold Cup Never qualified

Current Results

📎 **It is highly likely that the inhabitants of Belize could take less pleasure in football than others. After all, their ancestors, the Mayas, practised much more exciting ball games. One involved striking a massive rubber ball weighing about a kilogram. Experts are split on whether only the losers or both losers and winners were executed after the game.**

BARBADOS / CONCACAF

154th (144 points) ↑↓

🏳 Barbados Football Association

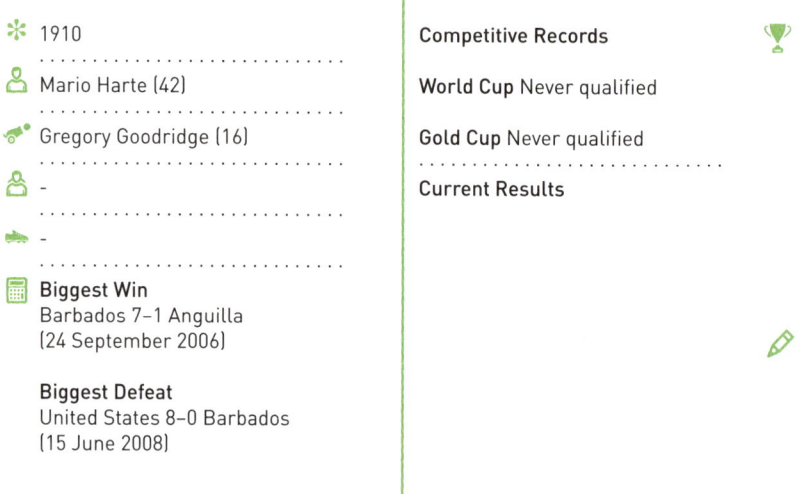

❉ 1910

👤 Mario Harte (42)

⚽ Gregory Goodridge (16)

👤 -

🚌 -

🗓 **Biggest Win**
Barbados 7–1 Anguilla
(24 September 2006)

Biggest Defeat
United States 8–0 Barbados
(15 June 2008)

Competitive Records 🏆

World Cup Never qualified

Gold Cup Never qualified

Current Results

📎 'First, there was no luck, then bad luck.' This was probably in the minds of the Barbadian players after qualifying for the World Cup in 1978. When they played against Trinidad and Tobago, there had been both a loss and a win so a third game was needed to bring about a decider. Barbados happened to lose that one and were so dismayed that they did not even bother with the next three qualifying competitions.

CANADA / CONCACAF

94th (369 points) ⇅

🏳 **Canadian Soccer Association**

❄ 1912

👤 Julian de Guzmán (89)

🎯 Dwayne De Rosario (22)

👤 Yes

👕 Umbro

🧮 **Biggest Win**
St. Lucia 0–7 Canada
(7 October 2011)

Biggest Defeat
Mexico 8–0 Canada
(18 June 1993)

Competitive Records 🏆

World Cup Appearances 1
Group stage 1986

Gold Cup Appearances 15
Champions 1985, 2000

Current Results

📎 **The Canadians participated in their first, albeit unofficial, international match in 1885, losing 1–0 to the United States. Nearly 20 years later, they became Olympic champions in St. Louis. And that was about it! As a rule, the team do not score a lot of goals, but at least their next best feat for the following hundred years would be to reach the World Cup finals in 1986, from which they were promptly eliminated in the group stage.**

CAYMAN ISLANDS / CONCACAF

🌐

202nd (13 points) ⇅

🏴 Cayman Islands Football Association

✳ 1921

👤 Lee Ramoon

🎯 Lee Ramoon (12)

👤 Yes

👟 Umbro

🗒 **Biggest Win**
Cayman Islands 5–0 British Virgin
Islands (2 March 1994)

Biggest Defeat
Cuba 7–0 Cayman Islands
(6 September 2006)

Competitive Records 🏆

World Cup Never qualified

Gold Cup Never qualified

Current Results

🖉

📎 **This archipelago in the Caribbean is much better known as a financial centre than for its football prowess. While the billions stack up in the largest hedge fund location in the world, the national team's account looks badly in the black. On the credit side so far only a fourth place in the Caribbean Championship has been achieved.**

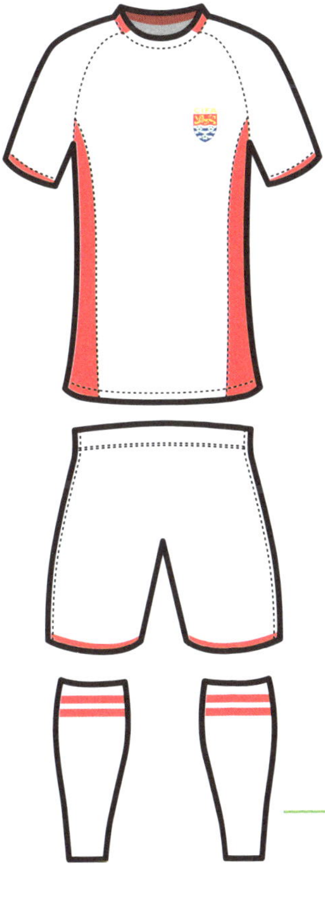

COSTA RICA / CONCACAF

26th (850 points)

⚑ Federación Costarricense de Fútbol

✳ 1921

👤 Walter Centeno (137)

⚽ Rolando Fonseca (47)

👤 Yes

👟 Lotto

🗓 **Biggest Win**
Costa Rica 12–0 Puerto Rico
(10 December 1946)

Biggest Defeat
Mexico 7–0 Costa Rica
(17 August 1975)

Competitive Records 🏆

World Cup Appearances 5
Quarter-finals 2014
Qualified for 2018*

Gold Cup Appearances 18
Champions 1963, 1969, 1989

Copa America Appearances 5
Quarter-finals 2001, 2004

Current Results

📎 **Anyone who wants to experience an emotional roller-coaster ride needs to watch a penalty shoot-out. There is no place on earth where heaven and hell are to be found closer. At the 2014 World Cup, Costa Rica experienced both. First, they beat Greece on penalties in the first knock-out round to put them on cloud nine. Then, when the next penalty drama came in the quarter-finals, Ruiz and Umaña experienced the hell of missing, thus sending Holland through cheering, while their side went home in tears.**

* Kit as far as known 3 January 2018

CUBA / CONCACAF

170th (98 points) ↑↓

🏳 Asociación de Fútbol de Cuba

✳ 1924

....

👤 Yénier Márquez (126)

....

⚽ Lester Moré (29)

....

👤 -

....

👟 Joma

....

📇 **Biggest Win**
Cuba 9–0 Puerto Rico
(27 May 1995)

Biggest Defeat
Aruba 8–0 Cuba (19 August 1955);
Soviet Union 8–0 Cuba (24 July 1980)

Competitive Records 🏆

World Cup Appearances 1
Quarter-finals 1938

Gold Cup Appearances 10
Fourth place 1971

....

Current Results

✏

📎 **While some of the other national team squads are decimated in major tournaments by injured or suspended players, the Cuban team grumble about their shortage of players for other reasons. During their preparation for the 2012 Olympics in Canada, five of their players decided to defect.**

CURAÇAO / CONCACAF

84th (407 points) ↕

⚑ Federashon Futbòl Kòrsou

❋ 1921

👤 Ergilio Hato (35)

⚽ Felitciano Zschusschen (9)

👤 -

👟 -

🗒 **Biggest Win**
Curaçao 14–0 Puerto Rico
(21 December 1948)

Biggest Defeat
Netherlands 8–1 Curaçao
(23 April 1948)

Competitive Records 🏆

World Cup Never qualified

Gold Cup Never qualified

Current Results

This national team has not quite hit the heights that the eponymous blue liqueur made from bitter orange peel has. Nonetheless, the team, which only played its first game in 2011, has already won its first title. In 2017, the team beat Martinique and Jamaica, before celebrating as champions of the Caribbean Cup. Was Blue Curaçao their tipple of choice? We don't know.

1

2

DOMINICA / CONCACAF

⚑ Dominica Football Association

✳ 1970

👤 Glenson Prince (33)

⚽ Kurlson Benjamin (14)

👤 -

🚌 -

📅 **Biggest Win**
British Virgin Islands 0–10 Dominica
(15 October 2010)

Biggest Defeat
Mexico 10–0 Dominica
(19 June 2004)

Competitive Records 🏆

World Cup Never qualified

Gold Cup Never qualified

Current Results

🖉

📎 Even if there is one centenarian for every 3,450 inhabitants on this picturesque island, which is a mind-bogglingly high rate by international standards, not a single one of them can recollect a big football match. The national team could not even make it through the preliminary round of the Caribbean Nations Cup, not to mention the CONCACAF Gold Cup or, heaven forbid, the World Cup.

DOMINICAN REPUBLIC / CONCACAF

162nd (121 points)

⚑ Federación Dominicana de Fútbol

✴ 1953

👤 Jonathan Faña (38)

🔫 Jonathan Faña (20)

👤 -

🚌 Walon

📋 **Biggest Win**
Dominican Republic 17–0 British
Virgin Islands (14 October 2010)

Biggest Defeat
Trinidad and Tobago 9–0 Dominican
Republic (8 October 2008)

Competitive Records 🏆

World Cup Never qualified

Gold Cup Never qualified

Current Results

There are no football miracles to write home about here. That is down
to intense competition. It is not that the national football team is over-
whelmed by its neighbours. The opponent is a domestic one and it is
called baseball. Any interest in football habitually ends when the baseball season begins. Consequently, Dominicans remain pretty much
nonplussed when the national team is knocked out of tournaments.

GRENADA / CONCACAF

160th (132 points)

⚑ Grenada Football Association

❄ 1924

....

👤 Shalrie Joseph (16)

....

⚽ Ricky Charles (37)

....

👤 -

....

👕 Admiral

....

🖩 **Biggest Win**
Grenada 14–1 Anguilla
(15 April 1998)

Biggest Defeat
Trinidad and Tobago 7–0 Grenada
(5 June 1999)

Competitive Records 🏆

World Cup Never qualified

Gold Cup Appearances 2
Group stage 2009, 2011

....

Current Results

This Caribbean island nation first became known around the world following its invasion by American troops in 1983. The Grenada national side are nicknamed the 'Spice Boys' after the indigenous delicacies. Up till now, they have only managed two runners-up places in the Caribbean Cup.

GUATEMALA / CONCACAF

129th (242 points) ⇅

🏳 Federación Nacional de Fútbol de Guatemala

✳ 1961

👤 Carlos Ruiz (133)

📣 Carlos Ruiz (68)

👤 -

👟 Umbro

🗓 **Biggest Win**
Guatemala 10–1 Honduras
(14 September 1921)

Biggest Defeat
Costa Rica 9–1 Guatemala
(24 July 1955)

Competitive Records 🏆

World Cup Never qualified

Gold Cup Semi-finals 2007

Current Results

The tropical rainforest, largely covering the northern part of the country, is seriously threatened by a universal disrespect for the preservation of natural resources. The Guatemalan national team pose no such danger, however. It could hardly be said that they have been pulling up any trees of their own. Perhaps their fourth place finish in the CONCACAF Gold Cup is the first ray of light filtering through the forest canopy.

GUYANA / CONCACAF

164th (117 points)

⌑ Guyana Football Federation

✳ 1902

👤 Walter Moore (62)

🎯 Nigel Codrington (18)

👤 -

🚌 Admiral

🧮 **Biggest Win**
Guyana 14–0 Anguilla
(16 April 1998)

Biggest Defeat
Mexico 9–0 Guyana
(2 December 1987)

Competitive Records 🏆

World Cup Never qualified

Gold Cup Never qualified

Current Results

 With the large number of states associated with the word Guyana, such as British Guyana, Dutch Guyana and French Guyana, a Guyana Championship might be worth considering. Maybe the Guyana without a colonial epithet could win that one. So far, fourth place in the Caribbean Cup is the sum of what this outfit has achieved.

HAITI / CONCACAF

57th (607 points)

Fédération Haïtienne de Football

1904
....
Emmanuel Sanon (100)
....
Emmanuel Sanon (47)
....
-
....
Saeta
....
Biggest Win
Haiti 11–0 US Virgin Islands
(24 November 2004)

Biggest Defeat
Brazil 9–1 Haiti (30 August 1959);
Costa Rica 8–0 Haiti (19 March 1961)

Competitive Records

World Cup Appearances 1
First group stage 1974

Gold Cup Appearances 13
Champions 1973
Quarter-finals 2002, 2009
....
Current Results

The results of Haiti's sole participation in the World Cup in Munich back in 1974 were rather disappointing. After three defeats, they were eliminated in the first round. They did manage to score against Italy however, thereby ending the opposition goalkeeper's impressive clean sheet record. Dino Zoff had gone unbeaten in international matches for almost two years. After the brief optimism of going ahead against the 1970 runners-up, Haiti proceeded to concede three goals and no sooner could they utter the name of Emmanuel Sanon, their star forward, than their fans found themselves heading home.

HONDURAS / CONCACAF

70th (521 points) ⇅

🏳 Federación Nacional Autónoma de Fútbol de Honduras

✳ 1951

. . . .

👤 Maynor Figueroa (145)

. . . .

⚽ Carlos Pavón (57)

👤 -

. . . .

👟 Joma

. . . .

🧮 **Biggest Win**
Honduras 10–0 Nicaragua
(13 March 1946)

Biggest Defeat
Guatemala 10–1 Honduras
(14 September 1921)

Competitive Records 🏆

World Cup Appearances 3
(First) group stage 1982, 2010, 2014

Gold Cup Appearances 18
Champions 1981

. . . .

Current Results

✏

📎 This country has been causing a bit of a stir both off (see El Salvador) and on the field. Honduras qualified for the World Cup finals three times and won both the UNCAF Nations Cup and the Copa Centroamericana twice. Honduras celebrated their biggest win in 2011 when they beat Brazil 2–0 in the Copa America quarter-finals.

JAMAICA / CONCACAF

54th (625 points)

🏳 Jamaica Football Federation

* 1910

....

👤 Ian Goodison (128)

....

🥅 Luton Shelton (35)

👤 -

....

🚍 Romai

....

📋 **Biggest Win**
Jamaica 12–0 St. Martin
(24 November 2004)

Biggest Defeat
Costa Rica 9–0 Jamaica
(24 February 1999)

Competitive Records

World Cup Appearances 1
Group stage 1998

Gold Cup Appearances 11
Runners-up 2015, 2017

....

Current Results

📎 '**No Woman No Cry**' is often wrongly referred to as a reggae song for men missing a woman. The whole notion of crying comes in handy when it comes to the national football team also, who have an uncanny knack of making their fans cry when the 'Reggae Boyz' regularly exit tournaments in the early stages. At least their six Caribbean Cup titles have brought their fans tears of joy.

ST. LUCIA / CONCACAF

🌐

174th (97 points) ↕

🏳 St. Lucia Football Association

❄ 1979
....

👤 Kurt Frederick (26)
....

⚽ Kurt Frederick (5)
....

👤 -
....

🚌 -
....

📅 **Biggest Win**
St. Lucia 14–0 US Virgin Islands
(14 April 2001)

Biggest Defeat
St. Vincent and Grenadines 8–0
St. Lucia (1 October 2006)

Competitive Records 🏆

World Cup Never qualified

Gold Cup Never qualified
....

Current Results

✏

📎 This tiny island nation in the Caribbean was named after St. Lucy of Syracuse because, as legend has it, some French sailors were shipwrecked here on her name day in 1502. Lucy is the patron saint of poor, penitent prostitutes and sick children, but she would appear to have little to do with football, otherwise the national team might not so consistently fail to qualify for the big tournaments.

MEXICO / CONCACAF

16th (1032 points)

Federación Mexicana de Fútbol Asociación

1927

Claudio Suárez (178)

Javier Hernández (49)

Yes

Adidas

Biggest Win
Mexico 13–0 Bahamas
(28 April 1987)

Biggest Defeat
England 8–0 Mexico
(10 May 1961)

Competitive Records

World Cup Appearances 16
Quarter-finals 1970, 1986
Qualified for 2018*

Gold Cup Appearances 22
Champions 1965, 1971, 1977, 1993,
1996, 1998, 2003, 2009, 2011, 2015

Current Results

Mexico's 2018 World Cup story is pretty much a given. Their national side will go out in the last 16. Why should anything be any different in 2018 considering that this has been their fate in the last six World Cups?

274

* Kit as far as known 3 January 2018

MONTSERRAT / CONCACAF

198th (20 points) ↑↓

🏳 Montserrat Football Association

✳ 1994

👤 Calvin Etrie (5)

⚽ Jaylee Hodgson (8)

👤 -

👕 -

🗓 **Biggest Win**
British Virgin Islands 0–7 Montserrat
(9 September 2012)

Biggest Defeat
Bermuda 13–0 Montserrat
(29 February 2004)

🏆 Competitive Records

World Cup Never qualified

Gold Cup Never qualified

Current Results

✏

📎 When a volcano erupted in 1995, the island was so badly damaged that almost all games now have to be played outside of the country. One game in particular will go down in history. The Dutch failed to qualify for the 2002 World Cup in Japan and South Korea, so Johan Kramer and Matthijs de Jongh from the Dutch ad agency Kessels Kramer organised an alternative. As the real final took place between Germany and Brazil in Yokohama, last placed Montserrat played against second last, Bhutan losing 4–0 in Thimphu in the Himalayas. The game was made famous in the 2003 film *The Other Final*.

1

2

NICARAGUA / CONCACAF

106th (315 points) ⇅

🏴 Federación Nicaragüense de Fútbol

* 1931
....
👤 David Solorzano (49)
....
⚽ Emilio Palacios (11)
....
👤 Yes
....
🚑 -
....

📅 **Biggest Win**
Nicaragua 5–0 Anguilla (23 March
2015); Nicaragua 5–0 Cuba
(8 December 2015)

Biggest Defeat
Honduras 10–0 Nicaragua (13 March
1946); Netherlands Antilles 11–1
Nicaragua (2 March 1950)

Competitive Records 🏆

World Cup Never qualified

Gold Cup Group stage 2009
....
Current Results

📎 **When the most feared opponent is called the Netherlands Antilles,
then it says everything about the state of soccer in Nicaragua. They
have already lost three times to the team rooted to the bottom of the
world rankings. And when it came to the qualifying games against the
underdogs of the Netherlands Antilles for the 2010 World Cup, Nicaragua lost twice again and without scoring a single goal.**

1

2

PANAMA / CONCACAF

56th (621 points)

Federación Panameña de Fútbol

1937
....

Gabriel Gómez (140)
....

Luis Tejada (43)
....

-
....

New Balance
....

Biggest Win
Panama 12–1 Puerto Rico
(13 December 1946)

Biggest Defeat
Panama 0–11 Costa Rica
(16 February 1938)

Competitive Records

World Cup
Qualified for 2018* (first time)

Gold Cup Appearances 8
Runners-up 2005, 2013
....

Current Results

The fact that big football stars are mentioned in the same breath as Panama has little to do with sport and more to do with the so-called 'Panama Papers'. Several major names cropped up in documents leaked to German newspaper *Süddeutsche Zeitung*, exposing a bunch of football high-rollers squirrelling away their eye-watering earnings to this offshore tax haven. No doubt some of the football world's talented tax-evaders passed on useful footballing tips to the locals during their clandestine visits. Once they'd deposited their wads of cash, they must have given a few coaching sessions, because the national team, at one stage, reached the lofty heights of 38th in the world rankings.

PUERTO RICO / CONCACAF

165th (112 points) ⇅

🏳 Federación Puertorriqueña de Fútbol

❇ 1940
....

👤 Andrés Cabrero (33), Héctor Ramos (33)
....

⚽ Héctor Ramos (18)
....

👤 Yes
....

👟 Nike
....

📅 **Biggest Win**
Puerto Rico 9–0 St. Martin
(9 September 2012)

Biggest Defeat
Netherlands Antilles 15–0 Puerto Rico
(7 January 1959)

Competitive Records 🏆

World Cup Never qualified

Gold Cup Never qualified
....

Current Results

📎 **This US foreign territory is not the typical dream destination for footballing stadium hoppers. You'd be more likely to visit for sports such as volleyball and surfboarding, which are far more popular here than soccer. Their heaviest defeat came in Venezuela in 1959 when they lost 15–0 to the Netherlands Antilles – not widely regarded as a football superpower themselves.**

ST. KITTS AND NEVIS / CONCACAF

113rd (291 points)

🏴 St. Kitts and Nevis Football Association

✳ 1932

👤 Atiba Harris (56)

🔫 Atiba Harris (14)

👤 -

🚐 -

🧮 **Biggest Win**
St. Kitts and Nevis 10–0 Montserrat
(17 April 1992)

Biggest Defeat
Mexico 8–0 St. Kitts and Nevis
(17 November 2004)

Competitive Records 🏆

World Cup Never qualified

Gold Cup Never qualified

Current Results

📎 This federation of two islands is a sovereign state belonging to the Lesser Antilles chain. It is perhaps more noted for its music than its football. Joan Armatrading was born here. Some say that her album *Into the Blues* may well have been inspired by the national team, whose inept performances have been known to give their fans the blues. In fact, come to think of it, many of her hits have a football theme – 'Down to Zero', 'Show Some Emotion' and 'The Game of Love', for example.

EL SALVADOR / CONCACAF

100th (352 points) ⇅

🚩 Federación Salvadoreña de Fútbol

❊ 1935

👤 Alfredo Pacheco (88)

⚽ Raúl Díaz Arce (39)

👤 Yes

👟 Umbro

🗓 **Biggest Win**
El Salvador 12–0 Anguilla
(6 February 2008)

Biggest Defeat
Hungary 10–1 El Salvador
(15 June 1982)

Competitive Records 🏆

World Cup Appearances 2
(First) group stage 1970, 1982

Gold Cup Appearances 15
Runners-up 1963, 1981

Current Results

📎 Some people refer to football as 'war' and the Salvadoreans are not entirely guiltless on that score. On 26 June 1969, Pipo Rodriguez scored the winning goal that knocked Honduras out of the World Cup qualifications for Mexico 1970. This triggered armed conflict lasting one hundred hours between the two countries, which went down in history as the 'football war'.

SURINAME / CONCACAF

128th (245 points) ⇅

🏳 Surinaamse Voetbal Bond

✳ 1920

👤 Marlon Felter (44)

⚽ Stefano Rijssel (10)

👤 -

👕 -

🧮 **Biggest Win**
Suriname 9–0 French Guiana
(2 March 1947)

Biggest Defeat
Mexico 8–1 Suriname (15 October
1977); Costa Rica 7–0 Suriname
(6 September 2008)

Competitive Records 🏆

World Cup Never qualified

Gold Cup Never qualified

Current Results

📎 **Suriname would have been a genuine wonder of the modern football world, had their great talents not pledged their allegiance to the KNVB. Ruud Gullit, Frank Rijkaard, Edgar Davids, Clarence Seedorf, Patrick Kluivert and others chose to compete for the motherland of this former colony and, in so doing, went on to achieve tremendous success for Holland.**

288

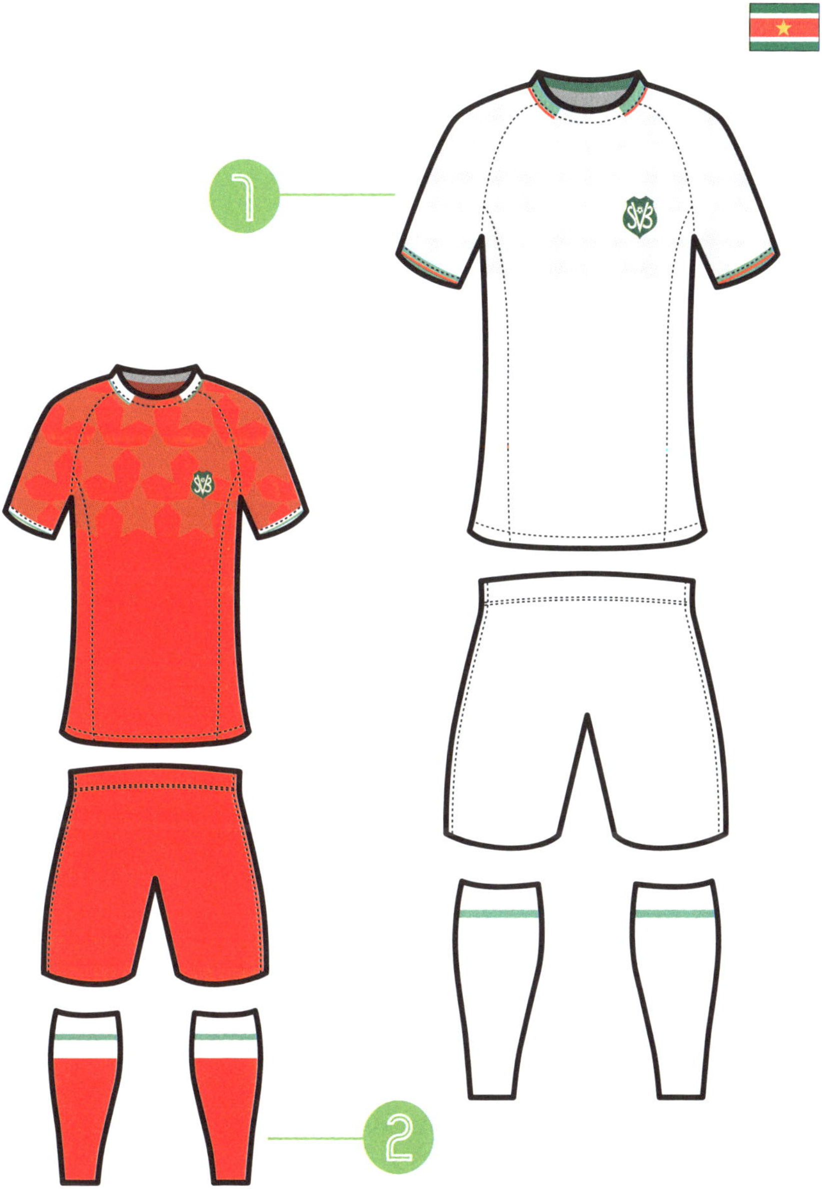

TURKS AND CAICOS ISLANDS / CONCACAF

TCIFA
Turks and Caicos Islands Football Association

TCA

202nd (13 points)

Turks and Caicos Islands Football Association

1996

Philip Shearer (14)

Gavin Glinton (4)

-

Admiral

Biggest Win
Cayman Islands 0–2 Turks and Caicos Islands (4 September 2006);
British Virgin Islands 0–2 Turks and Caicos Islands (4 June 2014)

Biggest Defeat
St. Kitts and Nevis 8–0 Turks- and Caicos Islands (18 March 2000)

Competitive Records

World Cup Never qualified

Gold Cup Never qualified

Current Results

There is no easy way to say this, but the football played by these Caribbean islands is pants. Even if we disregard the two easy 2–0 wins over minnows the Cayman Islands and the British Virgin Islands, they tend to lose a lot and usually by a hefty margin.

TRINIDAD AND TOBAGO / CONCACAF

89th (402 points) ⇅

🏳 Trinidad and Tobago Football Federation

❄ 1908

👤 Angus Eve (117)

🎯 Stern John (70)

👤 Yes

🚚 Joma

📅 **Biggest Win**
Trinidad and Tobago 11–0 Aruba
(4 June 1989)

Biggest Defeat
Mexico 7–0 Trinidad and Tobago
(8 October 2000)

Competitive Records 🏆

World Cup Appearances 1
Group stage 2006

Gold Cup Appearances 15
Runners-up 1973

Current Results

✐

📎 Hats off to this national team. Trinidad and Tobago is one of the smallest countries to have ever qualified for the finals of a World Cup. And their showing at the finals in Germany 2006 was more than respectable. Even with a man sent off, they defied the Swedes to earn a 0–0 draw. Following that they narrowly missed out against both England and Paraguay.

USA / CONCACAF

24th (867 points)

🏳 United States Soccer Federation

❄ 1913

....

👤 Cobi Jones (164)

....

⚽ Clint Dempsey (57), Landon Donovan (57)

....

👤 Yes

....

👟 Nike

....

🖩 **Biggest Win**
USA 8–0 Barbados
(15 June 2008)

Biggest Defeat
Norway 11–0 USA
(11 August 1948)

Competitive Records 🏆

World Cup Appearances 10
Third place 1930

Gold Cup Appearances 16
Champions 1991, 2002, 2005, 2007,
2015, 2017

....

Current Results

📎 Why is football not popular in the United States? The answer to that is, many Americans will tell you, it is boring. There are not enough goals scored. However, in the US national team's first international match, there were five. In 1916, the United States' 3–2 victory against Sweden was the first encounter between two teams from different continents. A few years ago, soccer, as it is known, ranked below monster trucks, frisbee and cheerleading in a list of America's most popular spectator sports. However, in the wake of it being played in schools, it has risen to number five on that list. And the US's 1–0 win over England at the 1950 World Cup in Brazil is probably best not mentioned here.

BRITISH VIRGIN ISLANDS / CONCACAF

205th (6 points) ⇅

⚑ British Virgin Islands Football Association

✳ 1974

👤 Andy Davis (14)

🔫 Avondale Williams (5)

👤 -

👟 Adidas

🧮 **Biggest Win**
British Virgin Islands 5–0 US Virgin Islands (30 January 2004)

Biggest Defeat
Dominican Republic 17–0 British Virgin Islands (14 October 2010)

Competitive Records 🏆

World Cup Never qualified

Gold Cup Never qualified

Current Results

📎 The greatest claim to fame for this British overseas dependency in the Caribbean is that it was able to afford its neighbouring, and equally unsuccessful, American Virgin Islands' football team two victories. Wins of their own are rare, but they did at least raise a smile when they beat the USVI 5–0 at home in 2004. Several players are drawn from the English non-league scene and represent such mighty outfits as Leek, Chippenham, Nantwich Town and Kidsgrove Athletic.

ST. VINCENT AND THE GRENADINES / CONCACAF

169th (99 points) ⇅

🏳 St. Vincent and The Grenadines Football Federation

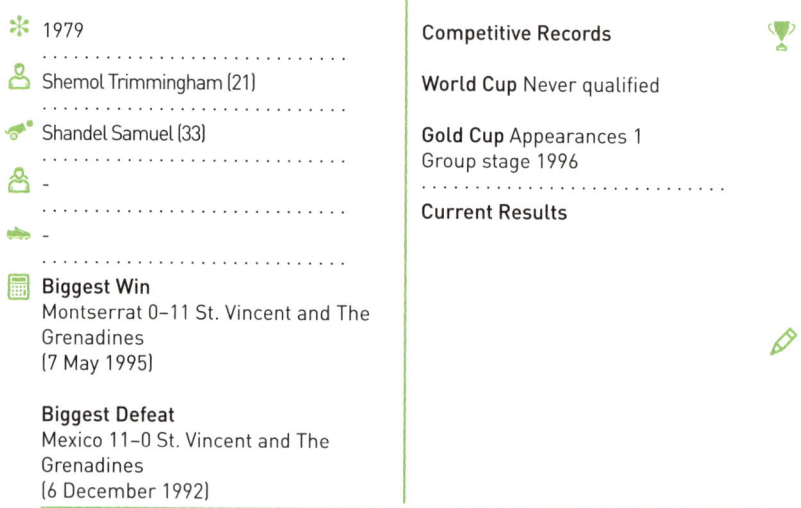

✳ 1979

....

👤 Shemol Trimmingham (21)

....

🔫 Shandel Samuel (33)

👤 -

....

🚑 -

....

🖩 **Biggest Win**
Montserrat 0–11 St. Vincent and The
Grenadines
(7 May 1995)

Biggest Defeat
Mexico 11–0 St. Vincent and The
Grenadines
(6 December 1992)

Competitive Records 🏆

World Cup Never qualified

Gold Cup Appearances 1
Group stage 1996

....

Current Results

📎 **Whilst it might sound like a 1950s doo-wop group, this chain of tiny islands is more like a cutting-edge techno DJ. There are more mobile phones than inhabitants in this Caribbean state, but it is unlikely they are being used to chat about football. Although the national team are rated as one of the stronger sides in the Caribbean, the most they have achieved so far is a second place in the Caribbean Cup.**

US VIRGIN ISLANDS / CONCACAF

197th (26 points) ⇅

🏳 U.S. Virgin Islands Soccer Federation

✳ 1989

👤 Dusty Good (9)

🔫 Kevin Sheppard (2), Reid Klopp (2)

👤 -

🚌 Admiral

📅 **Biggest Win**
US Virgin Islands 2–0 British Virgin Islands (3 July 2011)

Biggest Defeat
St. Lucia 14–1 US Virgin Islands (14 April 2001)

Competitive Records 🏆

World Cup Never qualified

Gold Cup Never qualified

Current Results

These islands were at one time a joyful discovery for Christopher Columbus. Football fans are somewhat less forthcoming when it comes to this cluster of islands and US foreign territory in the Caribbean. An overall goal difference of 17 scored and 160 conceded does not sound particularly promising. They do, however, command respect from neighbours the British Virgin Islands, whom they have beaten twice.

CONMEBOL

- CONMEBOL -

The South American Football Confederation was founded as early as 1916. This is by far the oldest of the continental associations, yet with only ten member countries it is also the smallest. Nonetheless, its national teams have still managed to win nine World Cup titles. CONMEBOL's most important competition is the Copa América, which was first played in the year the confederation was founded. To facilitate the competition having three groups of four, two guest nations are invited to participate at every Copa.

ARGENTINA / CONMEBOL

4th (1349 points) ↕

⚑ Asociación del Fútbol Argentino

✳ 1893

👤 Javier Zanetti (143)

🔫 Lionel Messi (61)

👤 Yes

👟 Adidas

Biggest Win
Argentina 12–0 Ecuador
(22 January 1942)

Biggest Defeat
Argentina 0–5 Colombia (5 September
1993); Bolivia 6–1 Argentina
(1 April 2009)

Competitive Records 🏆

World Cup Appearances 17
Champions 1978, 1986
Qualified for 2018*

Copa America Appearances 41
Champions 1921, 1925, 1927, 1929,
1937, 1941, 1945, 1946, 1947, 1955,
1957, 1959, 1991, 1993

Current Results

📎 This is a tragedy of almost Shakespearean proportions: Lionel Messi is one of the foremost football geniuses of all time, yet he will forever be second best in the country of his birth. And that is all to do with Maradona. There was even an attempt to stop Maradona's number 10 shirt number from ever being used again, but that was rejected, meaning Messi can now step into the rather sizeable shoes of the great Diego.

* Kit as far as known 3 January 2018

BOLIVIA / CONMEBOL

49th (672 points)

🏳 Federación Boliviana de Fútbol

✳ 1925

👤 Ronald Raldes (99)

🔫 Joaquín Botero (20)

👤 Yes

👟 Marathon Sports

📅 **Biggest Win**
Bolivia 7–0 Venezuela (22 August 1993); Bolivia 9–2 Haiti (5 March 2000)

Biggest Defeat
Uruguay 9–0 Bolivia (6 November 1927);
Brazil 10–1 Bolivia (10 April 1949)

Competitive Records 🏆

World Cup Appearances 3
(First) group stage 1930, 1950, 1994

Copa Appearances 26
Champions 1963

Current Results

📎 Many fans dream of suffering top of the league vertigo. This is actually not ideal when it comes to playing away against Bolivia. The stadium in La Paz lies at 3,600 metres above sea level, which means the air for most opponents is very thin. Take Argentina for example. They took a 6–1 hammering at the hands of their Andean neighbours in a 2010 World Cup qualifier and are still trying to get over the altitude sickness.

BRAZIL / CONMEBOL

BRASIL

2nd (1483 points)

⌖ Confederação Brasileira de Futebol

1914

Cafu (142)

Pelé (77)

Yes

Nike

Biggest Win
Brazil 14–1 Nicaragua
(17 October 1975)

Biggest Defeat
Brazil 1–7 Germany
(8 July 2014)

Competitive Records

World Cup Appearances 21
Champions 1958, 1962, 1970, 1994,
2002
Qualified for 2018*

Copa America Appearances 35
Champions 1919, 1922, 1949, 1989,
1997, 1999, 2004, 2007

Current Results

Pelé, Garrincha, Ronaldo, Neymar and many more legends have made this distinctive yellow shirt famous. But few will realise that its designer, Aldyr Garcia Schlee, actually supports Uruguay. When he won the competition to design the new national football kit in 1953, Schlee was a 19-year-old illustrator working for his local newspaper in Pelotas near the Uruguayan border. He is now a prize-winning novelist. The shirt has seen Brazil crowned world champions on five occasions. After their third win in 1970, they were given the Jules Rimet trophy to keep in perpetuity.

* Kit as far as known 3 January 2018

CHILE / CONMEBOL

10th (1162 points)

🏳 **Federación de Fútbol de Chile**

✳ 1895

👤 Claudio Bravo (119)

⚽ Alexis Sánchez (39)

👤 Yes

🚌 Nike

🧮 **Biggest Win**
Chile 7–0 Venezuela (29 August 1979);
Chile 7–0 Armenia (4 January 1997);
Chile 7–0 Mexico (18 June 2016)

Biggest Defeat
Brazil 7–0 Chile
(17 September 1959)

🏆 **Competitive Records**

World Cup Appearances 9
Third place 1962

Copa America Appearances 38
Champions 2015, 2016

Current Results

📎 Some teams tend to be their own worst enemies and enemies don't come any worse than 'La Roja' – the glorious Chilean national team. An appeal to the sports tribunal gained the team two points after their opponents, Bolivia, fielded an ineligible player. However, Bolivia played the same trick against the Peruvians, who also profited from the verdict, receiving an additional three points. Then the arbitration committee decided to dock the points again from all three, which means that the 2018 World Cup is taking place without the likes of Claudio Bravo, Alexis Sanchez and Gary Medel.

COLOMBIA / CONMEBOL

13th (1078 points) ↑↓

🏳 Federación Colombiana de Fútbol

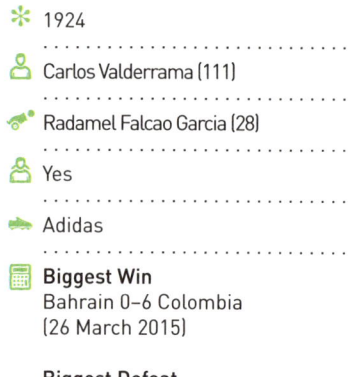

✳ 1924

👤 Carlos Valderrama (111)

⚽ Radamel Falcao Garcia (28)

👤 Yes

👟 Adidas

🖩 **Biggest Win**
Bahrain 0–6 Colombia
(26 March 2015)

Biggest Defeat
Brazil 9–0 Colombia
(24 March 1957)

Competitive Records 🏆

World Cup Appearances 6
Quarter-finals 2014
Qualified for 2018*

Copa America Appearances 21
Champions 2001

Current Results

📎 **Colombia travelled to the 1994 World Cup in the USA as many a punter's tip to win outright, but the tournament ended tragically for captain Valderrama's team after Andrés Escobar's own goal against the USA eliminated his team in the first round. Escobar was later shot dead in a bar in Medellín. There was speculation that the murderer had been sent by his namesake, infamous drug lord Pablo Escobar, but it turned out that Pablo had died a year earlier and, had the big soccer fan still been alive, Andres may never have been shot.**

* Kit as far as known 3 January 2018

ECUADOR / CONMEBOL

🌐

71st (508 points) ⇅

🏳 Federación Ecuatoriana de Fútbol

✳ 1925

👤 Iván Hurtado (168)

🎯 Agustín Delgado (31)

👤 -

🚍 Marathon Sports

📓 **Biggest Win**
Ecuador 6–0 Peru
(22 June 1975)

Biggest Defeat
Argentina 12–0 Ecuador
(22 January 1942)

Competitive Records 🏆

World Cup Appearances 3
Round of 16 2006

Copa America Appearances 27
Fourth place 1959, 1993

Current Results

✏

📎 **When Darwin visited the Galapagos Islands, which belong to Ecuador, he was fascinated by the turtles. These days, he would also need to observe the national team performances. It seems their evolution is going well. In 2013, they were in the world's top ten. The reason they did not make it any further was that Darwin's compatriot David Beckham scored the winner leading to Ecuador's elimination from the last 16 round of the 2006 World Cup.**

PARAGUAY / CONMEBOL

30th (812 points) ⇅

🏳 Asociación Paraguaya de Fútbol

❋ 1906
. . . .
👤 Paulo da Silva (144)
. . . .
🔫 Roque Santa Cruz (32)
. . . .
👤 -
. . . .
👟 Adidas
. . . .
📅 **Biggest Win**
Paraguay 7–0 Bolivia (30 April 1949);
Hong Kong 0–7 Paraguay (17 November 2010)

Biggest Defeat
Argentina 8–0 Paraguay
(20 October 1926)

Competitive Records 🏆

World Cup Appearances 8
Quarter-finals 2010

Copa America Appearances 34
Champions 1953, 1979
. . . .
Current Results

📎 So close, yet so ... Paraguay's golden generation set the world stage on fire between 1990 and the 2006 World Cup qualifiers. They bowed out from the last 16 twice and once in the quarters, each time getting beaten by just 1–0. Curiously, too, they were beaten twice by the team going on to become champions. In fact, the 1998 game with France ended in a golden goal shoot-out before Paraguay went out.

PERU / CONMEBOL

11st (1128 points)

Federación Peruana de Fútbol

1922

Roberto Palacios (128)

Paolo Guerrero (33)

Yes

Marathon Sports

Biggest Win
Peru 9–1 Ecuador
(11 August 1938)

Biggest Defeat
Brazil 7–0 Peru
(26 June 1997)

Competitive Records

World Cup Appearances 4
Quarter-finals 1970, last 8 1978
Qualified for 2018*

Copa America Appearances 29
Champions 1939, 1975

Current Results

Politicians cosying up to footballers is nothing new. What happened in Argentina during the World Cup finals of 1978 was very dubious. The hosts needed a big win against the Peruvians to go into the final. Among other top politicians, Henry Kissinger was presented to the team. Maybe he paved the way for Argentina to hammer Peru 6–0.

* Kit as far as known 3 January 2018

URUGUAY / CONMEBOL

21st (924 points) ⇅

🏳 ## Asociación Uruguaya de Fútbol

✳ 1900

👤 Maxi Pereira (123)

🎯 Luis Suárez (49)

👤 -

👟 Puma

🧮 **Biggest Win**
Uruguay 9–0 Bolivia
(9 November 1927)

Biggest Defeat
Uruguay 0–6 Argentina
(20 July 1902)

Competitive Records 🏆

World Cup Appearances 13
Champions 1930, 1950
Qualified for 2018*

Copa America Appearances 45
Champions 1916, 1917, 1920, 1923,
1924, 1926, 1935, 1942, 1956, 1959,
1967, 1983, 1987, 1995, 2011

Current Results ✏

📎 **Among the two-time world champions there is one player in particular who deserves a special mention. His name is Héctor Castro. As a 13-year-old he accidentally cut off his forearm with a chainsaw. He was nicknamed 'El Manco' or 'one arm', but he was far from 'armless for his national team. Quite the opposite in fact. The one-limbed wonder's goal gave Uruguay their first World Cup title in 1930.**

* Kit as far as known 3 January 2018

VENEZUELA / CONMEBOL

52nd (639 points)

🏳 Federación Venezolana de Fútbol

❄ 1926

👤 Juan Arango (129)

🔫 Juan Arango (23)

👤 Yes

🚚 Adidas

🧮 **Biggest Win**
Venezuela 7–0 Puerto Rico
(16 January 1959)

Biggest Defeat
Argentina 11–0 Venezuela
(10 August 1975)

Competitive Records 🏆

World Cup Never qualified

Copa America Appearances 17
Fourth place 2011

Current Results

📎 Many countries have issued travel warnings because of high crime rates and political instability in this country. For international football teams, however, there has really been little to be worried about. Venezuela is the only member of the South American Football Confederation that has never participated in the World Cup, which begs the question: how good did it feel to beat Brazil in 2008?

The Oceania Football Confederation is the newest of the continental associations. It was established back in 1966 but was not recognised by FIFA as an independent confederation until 1996. If the 14 national associations, three of them are not members of the world association. Qualifying for the World Cup finals is not straightforward as they are only granted a 'half' place. The winner of their most important tournament, the OFC Nations Cup, then has to beat a team from another confederation to book their ticket to the World Cup.

AMERICAN SAMOA / OFC

ASA

119th (38 points)

Football Federation American Samoa

1984

Nicky Salapu (16)

Duane Atualevao (3), Ramin Ott (3)

-

Nike

Biggest Win
American Samoa 2–0 Cook Islands
(4 September 2015)

Biggest Defeat
Australia 31–0 American Samoa
(11 April 2001)

Competitive Records

World Cup Never qualified

OFC Cup Never qualified

Current Results

Even small countries can write football history. Located in Oceania, this unincorporated territory in the South Pacific Ocean managed to accomplish a memorable feat: they capitulated against Australia by 31 goals to nil. To this day, it is the highest defeat of any national side. Perhaps two minor wins against Tonga and the Cook Islands may have saved their blushes but, considering football is only the third most popular sport behind American football and rugby and that there are only just over 50,000 inhabitants compared with over 24 million in Australia, the talent pool available to their manager can only be described as paltry.

COOK ISLANDS / OFC

192nd (38 points) ↑↓

🏳 Cook Islands Football Association

✳ 1971

👤 Tony Jamieson (18)

⚽ Mani (2), Te Miha (2), Mateariki (2)

👤 -

🚌 -

📅 **Biggest Win**
Cook Islands 4–1 Tuvalu (1 September 2007); Tonga 0–3 Cook Islands (31 August 2015)

Biggest Defeat
Tahiti 30–0 Cook Islands (2 September 1971)

Competitive Records 🏆

World Cup Never qualified

OFC Cup Appearances 2
Group stage 1998, 2000

Current Results

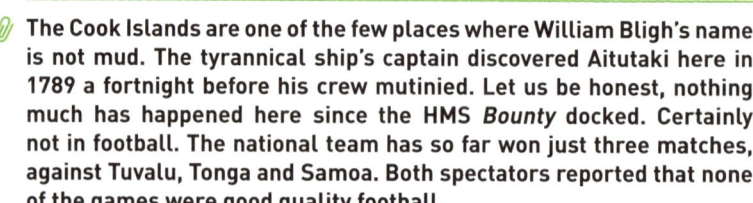

🖉 The Cook Islands are one of the few places where William Bligh's name is not mud. The tyrannical ship's captain discovered Aitutaki here in 1789 a fortnight before his crew mutinied. Let us be honest, nothing much has happened here since the HMS *Bounty* docked. Certainly not in football. The national team has so far won just three matches, against Tuvalu, Tonga and Samoa. Both spectators reported that none of the games were good quality football.

FIJI / OFC

178th (93 points)

🏳 Fiji Football Association

* 1961

👤 Esala Masi (52)

🎯 Esala Masi (33)

👤 -

👟 Kappa

🧮 **Biggest Win**
Fiji 24–0 Kiribati
(24 August 1979)

Biggest Defeat
New Zealand 13–0 Fiji
(16 August 1981)

Competitive Records 🏆

World Cup Never qualified

OFC Cup Appearances 7
Third place 1998, 2008

Current Results

📎 **They gave everything and came nowhere. During the 2002 World Cup qualifications, the Fiji players scored a whopping 27 goals in four games, but they were still unable to progress. In spite of resounding successes against American Samoa (13–0), Samoa (6–1) and Tonga (8–1), they were beaten by Australia (2–0), which led to their departure from the tournament.**

1

2

NEW CALEDONIA / OFC

156th (139 points) ⇅

🚩 Fédération Calédonienne de Football

※ 1928

👤 Pierre Wajoka (39)

⚽ Michel Hmaé (22)

👤 -

🚍 -

📅 **Biggest Win**
New Caledonia 18–0 Guam (3 September 1991); New Caledonia 18–0 Micronesia (1 July 2003)

Biggest Defeat
Australia 11–0 New Caledonia (Date unknown, 2002)

Competitive Records 🏆

World Cup Never qualified

OFC Cup Appearances 5
Runners-up 2008, 2012

Current Results

📎 **Even the greatest expert on the global soccer scene would need to think for a moment when quizzed on the subject of noteworthy footballing facts about New Caledonia. Here is a clue: the players of this island group in the Pacific won five times at the South Pacific Games, most recently with a 1–0 win over Fiji in 2007.**

NEW ZEALAND / OFC

NEW ZEALAND FOOTBALL

122nd (267 points) ⇅

🏴 New Zealand Football

✳ 1891

....

👤 Ivan Vicelich (88)

....

⚽ Vaughan Coveny (28)

....

👤 Yes

....

👕 Nike

....

🗓 **Biggest Win**
New Zealand 13–0 Fiji
(16 August 1981)

Biggest Defeat
New Zealand 0–10 Australia
(11 July 1936)

Competitive Records 🏆

World Cup Appearances 2
(First) group stage 1982, 2010

OFC Cup Appearances 10
Champions 1973, 1998, 2008, 2016

....

Current Results

📎 **Only one team remained unbeaten at the 2010 World Cup and it was not the eventual winner, Spain. It was the 'All Whites' from New Zealand, who played out three draws in the group stages, which was sadly not enough for them to progress into the knock-out rounds, but it was enough to finish above the Italians in the same group.**

1

2

NEW ZEALAND
FOOTBALL

PAPUA NEW GUINEA / OFC

161st (126 points) ⇅

🏳 **Papua New Guinea Football Association**

✳ 1962

👤 Richard Daniel (23)

📢 Reggie Davani (15)

👤 -

🚌 -

📅 **Biggest Win**
Papua New Guinea 20–0 American
Samoa (15 December 1987)

Biggest Defeat
Malaysia 10–1 Papua New Guinea
(June 1976); Australia 11–2 Papua
New Guinea (26 February 1980)

Competitive Records 🏆

World Cup Never qualified

OFC Cup Appearances 4
Runners-up 2016

Current Results

📎 **Considering that rugby league is the most popular sport, closely followed by Australian rules football and rugby union, putting an association football team together seems a task as daunting as searching for lost tribes in the impenetrable New Guinea Highlands. When it comes to which, most of us would tend to think of head hunters, not great headers of the ball; turtle poachers, not poachers in the six-yard box. In the few tournaments PNG have contested, they have enjoyed no success.**

SAMOA / OFC

192nd (38 points) ↑↓

🏳 Football Federation Samoa

✳ 1968

👤 Desmond Fa'aiuaso (17)

🔫 Desmond Fa'aiuaso (7)

👤 -

👟 Adidas

🧮 **Biggest Win**
Samoa 8–0 American Samoa
(9 April 2001)

Biggest Defeat
Tahiti 13–0 Western Samoa
(13 July 1981)

🏆 **Competitive Records**

World Cup Never qualified

OFC Cup Appearances 2
Group stage 2012, 2016

Current Results

📎 Before any criticism is levelled at the national team, please bear in mind that Samoa is the home to a very nasty wrestler known as Samoa Joe. Together with 50 active fellow members, he belongs to one of the world's biggest wrestling clans. The national team is certainly not as bad as the statistics would seem to point out. Erm, honest, Joe!

SOLOMON ISLANDS / OFC

148th (179 points) ↕

🏳 Solomon Islands Football Federation

❋ 1978

👤 Henry Fa'arodo (56)

🎯 Commins Menapi (34)

👤 -

👟 Adidas

📅 **Biggest Win**
Solomon Islands 17–0 Wallis and
Futuna (September 1991)

Biggest Defeat
Tahiti 18–0 Solomon Islands
(17 December 1963)

Competitive Records 🏆

World Cup Never qualified

OFC Cup Appearances 5
Runners-up 2004

Current Results

📎 **Although the island state does not have much more than half a million inhabitants, its team once came close to a World Cup finals. In the end, they didn't make it to Germany in 2006, after being defeated by Australia in the deciding match.**

1

2

FRENCH POLYNESIA / TAHITI / OFC

153rd (149 points)

⚑ Fédération Tahitienne de Football

✳ 1989

👤 Angelo Tchen (30)

⚽ Félix Tagawa (14)

👤 -

👟 Nike

🗓 **Biggest Win**
Tahiti 30–0 Cook Islands
(2 September 1971)

Biggest Defeat
New Zealand 10–0 Tahiti
(4 June 2004); Spain 10–0 Tahiti
(20 June 2013)

Competitive Records 🏆

World Cup Never qualified

OFC Cup Appearances 8
Champions 2012

Current Results

📎 **Tahiti's players are incredibly hungry for goals. No other national team has won more frequently by a margin of 13 or more. The Cook Islands were hit hardest when they were crushed 30–0. Sometimes, Tahiti are a bit like chalk and cheese. They were beaten 10–0 by Spain, making them the record holder for the highest defeat of any team from Oceania playing against a team from another confederation.**

1

2

TONGA / OFC

206th (0 points)

Tonga Football Association

1965

Lafaele Moala (16)

Mark Uhatahi (3)

-

FBT

Biggest Win
Tonga 7–0 Micronesia
(5 July 2003)

Biggest Defeat
Australia 22–0 Tonga
(9 April 2001)

Competitive Records

World Cup Never qualified

OFC Cup Never qualified

Current Results

Everyone scratches their head when their team is stuck to the bottom of the table, and the association football team from this southern Pacific archipelago has indeed been stuck there for quite a while. Tonga's position in the alphabet might explain their lowly spot in the table. Had they kept their original name, The Friendly Islands, they might be much higher up the league. Likewise, if Tongans Billy Vunipola and Jonah Lomu had opted for footy over rugby as their code of choice, it would have been squeaky-bum time for any team facing their fearsome war-dance – the *kailo*.

VANUATU / OFC

185th (55 points) ⇅

🏳 Vanuatu Football Federation

✳ 1934

👤 Chikau Mansale (18)

⚽ Richard Iwai (19)

👤 -

🚗 -

🖩 **Biggest Win**
Vanuatu 18–0 Kiribati
(7 July 2003)

Biggest Defeat
New Zealand 9–0 New Hebrides
(19 September 1951)

Competitive Records 🏆

World Cup Never qualified

OFC Cup Appearances 8
Fourth place 1973, 2000, 2002, 2008

Current Results

📎 **Even today on the Pentecost Islands, bartering is still a common way to do business. Stories can even be exchanged for money at a set rate. The most profitable story seems to be the national team's sensational 4–2 win against New Zealand. Winning this game meant that Vanuatu ruined their superior rival's chances of participation in the 2006 World Cup in Germany.**

The official name for the this European confederation is Union of European Football Associations or Union des Associations Européennes de Football. Founded in Basel, Switzerland, in 1954, UEFA organises numerous tournaments, with the most important one being the European Championship or Euros, as it has latterly become known. From 2018, a new competition called the UEFA Nations League will be added. This will take place every two years and will be extended to the national teams of all member associations. There are currently 55, some of which are not located in Europe, such as Israel and Azerbaijan. Kosovo is the newest member, having joined up in 2016. Greenland is keen to get involved but any attempts have been unsuccessful due to no pitches existing on the main island.

ALBANIA / UEFA

62nd (553 points)

⚑ Federata Shqiptare e Futbollit

✳ 1930

👤 Lorik Cana (93)

🥅 Erjon Bogdani (18)

👤 Yes

👕 Macron

🖩 **Biggest Win**
Albania 5–0 Vietnam (12 February 2003); Albania 6–1 Cyprus (12 August 2009)

Biggest Defeat
Albania 0–12 Hungary
(24 September 1950)

Competitive Records 🏆

World Cup Never qualified

European Championship
Appearances 1
Group stage 2016

Current Results

📎 **It is not derogatory to consider Albania a football minnow. After all, minnows kill giants. Football's world superpowers tend to underestimate such teams. In fact, West Germany, having crushed Albania 6–0 in Dortmund eight months earlier, were unable to win in the Albanian capital in 1967, which meant they failed to qualify for the 1968 European Championship in Italy. The 'Disgrace in Tirana' was blamed on the dry-as-a-bone playing surface and the Austrian referee. But it's worth noting that the Albanian keeper, Koço Dinella, made over forty saves in that match.**

1

2

ANDORRA / UEFA

139th (215 points) ↑↓

🏳 Federació Andorrana de Futbol

✳ 1994
....
👤 Ildefons Lima (111)
....
⚽ Ildefons Lima (11)
....
👤 Yes
....
👕 Adidas
....

📅 **Biggest Win**
Andorra 2–0 Albania (17 April 2002);
San Marino 0–2 Andorra (22 February 2017)

Biggest Defeat
Czech Republic 8–1 Andorra (4 June 2005); Croatia 7–0 Andorra (7 October 2006)

🏆 **Competitive Records**

World Cup Never qualified

European Championship
Never qualified
....
Current Results

✏

📎 If a country's entire population can fit into one stadium, then one cannot always expect footballing miracles. Andorra's national team have only been competing in international competitions for around 20 years and not many miracles have been forthcoming. In qualifiers for major tournaments they have always propped up their group in last place with zero points.

ARMENIA / UEFA

90th (383 points)

⚑ Hajastani futboli federazia

❄ 1992

👤 Sargis Hovsepyan (132)

⚽ Henrikh Mkhitaryan (23)

👤 -

👟 Adidas

🧮 **Biggest Win**
Armenia 7–1 Guatemala
(28 May 2016)

Biggest Defeat
Chile 7–0 Armenia (4 January 1997);
Georgia 7–0 Armenia (30 March 1997)

Competitive Records 🏆

World Cup Never qualified

European Championship
Never qualified

Current Results

📎 **There are some countries that football experts never lose sleep over and Armenia is one of them. It may be that it is to do with their only being around since the end of the Soviet Union. The true history of the six qualifying competitions they have been involved in can be summed up in four words: Armenia always crash out. However, as the first country in the world to adopt Christianity as its official religion, they can always pray for better days.**

AUSTRIA / UEFA

AUT

29th (815 points)

Österreichischer Fußball-Bund

1904

Andreas Herzog (103)

Toni Polster (44)

Yes

Puma

Biggest Win
Austria 9–0 Malta
(30 April 1977)

Biggest Defeat
Austria 1–11 England
(8 June 1908)

Competitive Records

World Cup Appearances 7
Third place 1954

European Championship
Appearances 2
Group stage 2008, 2016

Current Results

As we know, football commentators can also become part of soccer folklore – think of Kenneth Wolstenholme's immortal line, 'They think it's all over. It is now,' for example or simply look up the entry for Norway. This was also the case with Edi Finger, who worked on the Austria vs. West Germany clash at the World Cup in Argentina in 1978, which is still known to this day as the 'Miracle of Cordoba'. Austria won the game 3–2 and their winning strike prompted the delirious Finger into a momentous outpouring of unmitigated joy. In his thick Austrian accent, he declared, 'This is daft, daft, daft. I'm going daft, me.' during the game against the world champions and mighty neighbours.

AZERBAIJAN / UEFA

AFFA

117th (281 points) ↕

⚐ Association of Football Federations of Azerbaijan

✳ 1992
....
👤 Rasad Sadıqov (111)
....
🔫 Qurban Qurbanov (14)
....
👤 Yes
....
🚍 Umbro
....

🖩 **Biggest Win**
Azerbaijan 4–0 Liechtenstein (5 June
1999); Azerbaijan 5–1 San Marino
(4 September 2017)

Biggest Defeat
France 10–0 Azerbaijan
(6 September 1995)

Competitive Records 🏆

World Cup Never qualified

European Championship
Never qualified
....
Current Results

📎 I wonder what it feels like to have won the World Cup as a player; to
have reached the final of the Euros as a manager; and yet not to qualify
for a single tournament coaching the same team for six years. Former
West German international Berti 'Sexy Legs' Vogts might be able to
let the cat out of the bag in that regard, but let's face it, who would
dare ask him? He's probably enjoying the tea and bakhlava too much
anyway.

BELGIUM / UEFA

5th (1325 points) ↑↓

▭ Koninklijke Belgische Voetbalbond

✳ 1895

👤 Jan Vertonghen (97)

⚽ Paul Van Himst (30); Bernard Voorhoof (30)

👤 Yes

👟 Adidas

🖩 **Biggest Win**
Belgium 10–1 San Marino (28 February 2001); Belgium 9–0 Gibraltar (31 August 2017)

Biggest Defeat
England 6–1 Belgium (17 April 1909); Spain 5–0 Belgium (5 September 2009)

Competitive Records 🏆

World Cup Appearances 13
Fourth place 1986
Qualified for 2018*

European Championship
Runners-up 1980

Current Results

📎 **One of the most memorable experiences in Belgian football took place aboard a ship. In 1930, the team travelled on board the Italian ocean liner the *Conte Verde*, bound for the very first World Cup finals in Uruguay along with the national teams of Romania, France and Brazil, three referees, the World Cup trophy and FIFA President Jules Rimet himself. Whether their off-colour showing was down to their wobbly sea legs after the rough crossing cannot be said for certain, but the 1920 Olympic winners could not even manage to score a single goal in either of their games.**

* Kit as far as known 3 January 2018

BOSNIA AND HERZEGOVINA / UEFA

38th (753 points) ⇅

Nogometni/Fudbalski Savez Bosne i Hercegovine

1992

Emir Spahić (93)

Edin Džeko (52)

Yes

Adidas

Biggest Win
Liechtenstein 1–8 Bosnia and
Herzegovina (7 September 2012);
Bosnia and Herzegovina 7–0 Estonia
(10 September 2008)

Biggest Defeat
Argentina 5–0 Bosnia and Herzegovina (14 May 1998)

Competitive Records

World Cup Appearances 1
Group stage 2014

European Championship
Never qualified

Current Results

Many teams could be accused of lacking strength and grit, but the team of heavies that surrounds Edin Dzeko could be charged with nothing of the sort. During their World Cup 2018 qualifying clash with Greece, one of the Greek players lost two teeth. Fortunately, the team doctor found them lying around on the turf and restored them to the rightful owner, but any team would be advised to have gumshields at the ready if you are facing this bunch of battle-hardened toughs.

1

2

BELARUS / UEFA

🌐

92nd (372 points) ⇅

🏳 Belorusskaya Federatsiya Futbola

❊ 1989

👤 Aljaksandr Kulchy (102)

🔫 Maksim Romaschenko (20)

👤 Yes

🚐 Adidas

🧮 **Biggest Win**
Belarus 5–0 Lithuania (8 June 1998);
Belarus 6–1 Tajikistan (4 September 2014)

Biggest Defeat
Austria 5–0 Belarus
(11 June 2003)

Competitive Records 🏆

World Cup Never qualified

European Championship
Never qualified

Current Results

📎 **When one considers the general pandemonium made on reaching the top ten in the Eurovision Song Contest, the Belarus national team have in no way lived up to their singing counterparts on the international football stage. They did manage to beat Holland 2–1 during their first qualifying round for the Euros in 2007 and eked out a decent 2–2 draw against Germany in Kaiserslautern back in 2008, but a decade on and the White Wings don't have a lot to sing about.**

BULGARIA / UEFA

43rd (719 points) ⇅

🏳 Bulgarski futbolen sojus

✳ 1923

👤 Stiliyan Petrow (106)

🏹 Dimitar Berbatow (48)

👤 Yes

👟 Joma

🧮 **Biggest Win**
Bulgaria 10–0 Ghana
(14 October 1968)

Biggest Defeat
Spain 13–0 Bulgaria
(21 May 1933)

Competitive Records 🏆

World Cup Appearances 7
Fourth place 1994

European Championship
Appearances 2
Group stage 1996, 2004

Current Results

📎 **Even though football is a team sport, one single player can make all the difference and in 1994 that player was Hristo Stoichkov. At the World Cup that year, Bulgaria beat Argentina to then play against and knock out the reigning champions, Germany. Stoichkov paved the way with a marvellous free-kick. Sadly, the team went down to Italy in the semi-final.**

CROATIA / UEFA

17th (1018 points) ⇅

🚩 **Hrvatski nogometni savez**

✳ 1912

👤 Darijo Srna (134)

⚽ Davor Šuker (45)

👤 Yes

👟 Nike

🗓 **Biggest Win**
Croatia 10–0 San Marino
(4 June 2016)

Biggest Defeat
England 5–1 Croatia
(9 September 2009)

🏆 **Competitive Records**

World Cup Appearances 5
Third place 1998
Qualified for 2018*

European Championship
Appearances 5
Quarter-finals 1996, 2008

Current Results

📎 Croatia's rise in world football has been phenomenal. Shortly after Yugoslavia was disbanded, stars like Davor Šuker, Ivica Olić and Mario Mandžukić emerged, forcing their way into the world's top teams. Their success is also down to their indomitable spirit, embodied in the team's Verdan Corluka. Following a bloodied head injury at the 2016 Euros, the player caused a stir with his head bandage variations.

* Kit as far as known 3 January 2018

CYPRUS / UEFA

91st (373 points) ↕

⌂ Cyprus Football Association

❋ 1934

....

👤 Yiannakis Okkas (106)

....

🔫 Michalis Konstantinou (32)

....

👤 Yes

....

👟 Adidas

....

🖩 **Biggest Win**
Cyprus 5–0 Andorra (15 November 2000); Cyprus 5–0 Andorra (16 November 2014)

Biggest Defeat
West Germany 12–0 Cyprus (21 May 1969)

Competitive Records 🏆

World Cup Never qualified

European Championship
Never qualified

....

Current Results

🖉

📎 **Yet another minnow that relishes a giant-killing. In 1989, Cyprus drew against France, stopping them from qualifying for the 1990 World Cup. Their unlikely 3–2 win against Spain in the qualifiers for the 2000 World Cup led to Javier Clemente getting the boot. Reaching the finals of a major tournament continues to elude them, though.**

CZECH REPUBLIC / UEFA

🌐

48th (677 points) ⇅

🏳 Fotbalová asociace České republiky

❋ 1901

👤 Petr Čech (124)

💥 Jan Koller (55)

👤 Yes

🚚 Puma

🧮 **Biggest Win**
Czech Republic 7–0 San Marino
(9 September 2009)

Biggest Defeat
Russia 4–1 Czech Republic
(8 June 2012)

Competitive Records 🏆

World Cup Appearances 9
Runners-up 1934, 1962

European Championship
Appearances 9
Champions 1976

Current Results

✏

📎 **The Czech national side's greatest success was due to a 'Golden Goal' shoot-out. This is what proved decisive in the final of the Euros in 1996. The golden goal ruling was introduced to add excitement to knock-out ties ending drawn after 90 minutes. But the idea backfired, because both teams attempted to stop the other from scoring rather than going hell for leather to score. Eventually, in 2004, the golden goal was kicked into touch.**

DENMARK / UEFA

12nd (1099 points) ⇅

⚑ Dansk Boldspil-Union

❋ 1889

👤 Peter Schmeichel (129)

⚽ Poul Nielsen (52); Jon Dahl Tomasson (52)

👤 Yes

👕 Hummel

Biggest Win
Denmark 17–1 France
(22 October 1908)

Biggest Defeat
Germany 8–0 Denmark
(16 May 1937)

Competitive Records 🏆

World Cup Appearances 5
Quarter-finals 1998
Qualified for 2018*

European Championship
Appearances 8
Champions 1992

Current Results

When a tournament is not going their way, experts blame a team's preparation. Completely unprepared, this did not seem to stop Denmark from becoming the European champions in 1992. The country's players returned from their holidays at short notice due to Yugoslavia's disqualification and their own reinstatement. They then swept away their opponents. In later tournaments, the Danish Dynamite was not so explosive. The team were probably too well prepared.

* Kit as far as known 3 January 2018

ENGLAND / UEFA

🌐

15th (1047 points) ⇅

🏴 **The Football Association**

❄️ 1863

👤 Peter Shilton (125)

💥 Wayne Rooney (53)

👤 Yes

👟 Nike

🧮 **Biggest Win**
Ireland 0–13 England
(18 February 1882)

Biggest Defeat
Hungary 7–1 England
(23 May 1954)

Competitive Records 🏆

World Cup Appearances 15
Champions 1966
Qualified for 2018*

European Championship
Appearances 9
Third place 1968, 1996

Current Results

📎 **The match against Scotland in Glasgow on 30 November 1872 was the first international in the history of football. It ended 0–0. Many great inventors find to their regret that others profit far more from their ingenious idea than they themselves. Since inventing the sport, the motherland of football's 'Three Lions' have been crowned world champions only once. The eponymous 1996 song by The Lightning Seeds with Baddiel & Skinner contained the famous line, 'thirty years of hurt'. That song is now over 20 years old. Just saying.**

* Kit as far as known 3 January 2018

SPAIN / UEFA

6th (1231 points) ⇅

🏳 Real Federación Española de Fútbol

✳ 1913

👤 Iker Casillas (167)

🔫 David Villa (59)

👤 Yes

🚗 Adidas

🧮 **Biggest Win**
Spain 13–0 Bulgaria
(21 May 1933)

Biggest Defeat
Italy 7–1 Spain (4 June 1928);
England 7–1 Spain (9 December 1931)

Competitive Records 🏆

World Cup Appearances 15
Champions 2010
Qualified for 2018*

European Championship
Appearances 10
Champions 1964, 2008, 2012

Current Results

✏

📎 **It was the 'Maldición de Cuartos de Final' (the curse of the quarters) that made FIFA's founding member Spain wait over a century for success. Despite good performances, the Spanish team too often failed in the decisive rounds. But their lack of success came to an end in 2010, when Andrés Iniesta unleashed 'La Furia Roja' (the red fury) in the 116th minute of the World Cup final, scoring the winner to beat Holland 1–0 and finally hoist the coveted FIFA World Cup Trophy aloft in Johannesburg for Vicente del Bosque's side.**

* Kit as far as known 3 January 2018

ESTONIA / UEFA

84th (407 points)

Eesti Jalgpalli Liit

1921

Martin Reim (157)

Andres Oper (38)

Yes

Nike

Biggest Win
Estonia 6–0 Lithuania (26 July 1928);
Gibraltar 0–6 Estonia (7 October 2017)

Biggest Defeat
Finland 10–2 Estonia
(11 August 1922)

Competitive Records

World Cup Never qualified

European Championship
Never qualified

Current Results

What makes Estonia unique compared with national teams such as Germany, France and Holland? They boast an international player with 157 caps. Until 2009, Martin Reim was the player with the most caps in Europe. He was unfortunately unable to live up to his long-standing reputation at a major tournament and his team failed in the qualifications.

FINLAND / UEFA

67th (531 points) ⇅

🏳 Suomen Palloliitto

❄ 1907

👤 Jari Litmanen (137)

🔫 Jari Litmanen (32)

👤 Yes

👟 Nike

🧮 **Biggest Win**
Finland 8–0 San Marino
(17 November 2010)

Biggest Defeat
Germany 13–0 Finland
(1 September 1940)

Competitive Records 🏆

World Cup Never qualified

European Championship
Never qualified

Current Results

📎 Anyone looking for international success in Finnish football would have to delve back a long way in the history books. Over a hundred years to be exact. All those years ago, at the 1912 Olympic Games in Stockholm, Finland finished just short of the medal rankings in fourth place. Ice hockey is a far more popular sport in Finland.

FRANCE / UEFA

9th (1183 points) ⇅

▱ Fédération Française de Football

✳ 1919

👤 Lilian Thuram (142)

⚙ Thierry Henry (51)

👤 Yes

👟 Nike

📅 **Biggest Win**
France 10–0 Azerbaijan
(6 September 1995)

Biggest Defeat
Denmark 17–1 France
(19 October 1908)

Competitive Records 🏆

World Cup Appearances 15
Champions 1998
Qualified for 2018*

European Championship
Appearances 9
Champions 1984, 2000

Current Results

📎 A better example of effective integration would be difficult to find. With its perfect combination of 'black-blanc-beur' or better put 'black, white and berber' (referring to the many players of Maghreb origin), the Équipe Tricolore have chalked up some distinguished international triumphs. With France's three-time footballer of the world Zinédine Zidane and his Algerian roots, Les Bleus became the 1998 world and the 2000 European champions.

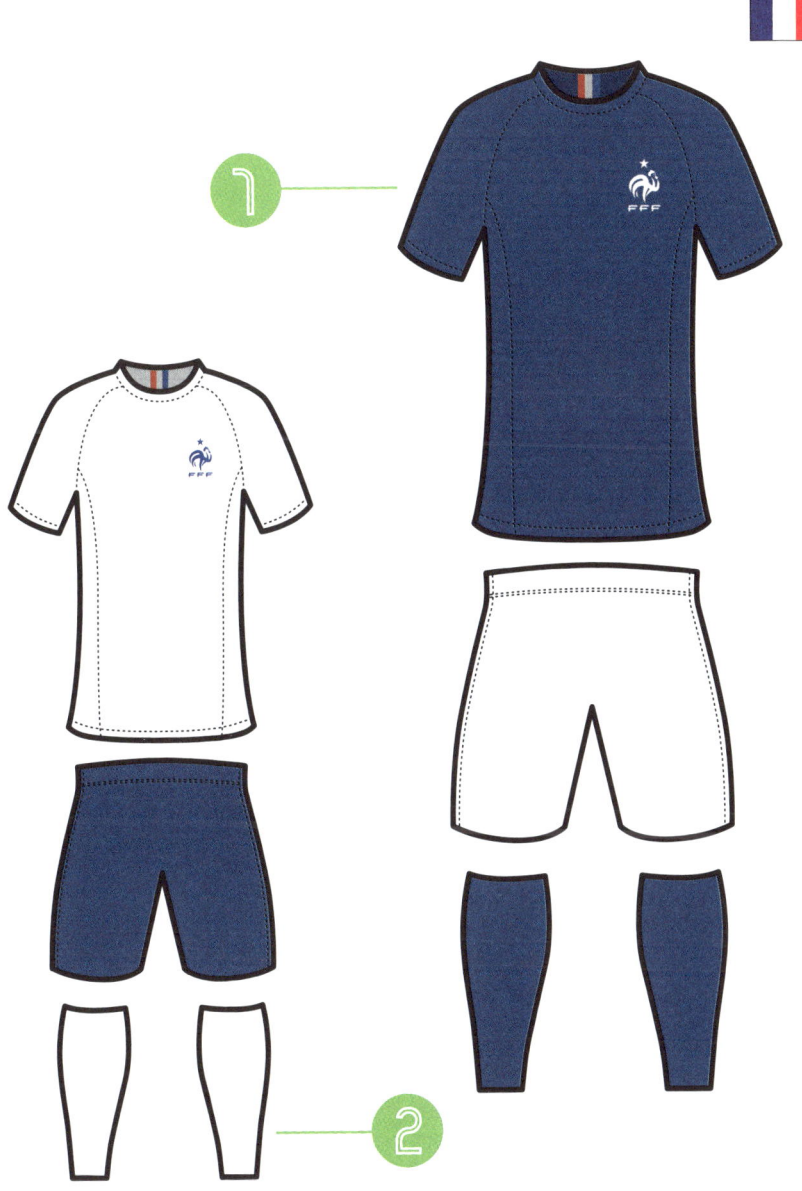

FAROE ISLANDS / UEFA

⊕

95th (364 points) ⇅

🏳 Fótbóltssamband Føroya

✳ 1979

👤 Fróði Benjaminsen (93)

🔫 Rógvi Jacobsen (10)

👤 Yes

👟 Adidas

🖩 **Biggest Win**
Faroe Islands 3–0 San Marino (25 May 1995); Gibraltar 1–4 Faroe Islands (1 March 2014)

Biggest Defeat
Faroe Islands 1–8 Federal Republic of Yugoslavia (6 October 1996)

Competitive Records 🏆

World Cup Never qualified

European Championship
Never qualified

Current Results

🖊

📎 **To steer clear of trouble in Austria, it is best to not mention the name of this country out loud. After all, people on this north Atlantic volcanic archipelago are outnumbered by sheep. In 1990, their players sheared the Austrian team of their woolly dignity by despatching them 1–0 in a European Championship qualifier. Even the mighty Germans have struggled to avoid embarrassment against the Faroes – they have only managed to beat them twice, with both games going very close.**

GEORGIA / UEFA

104th (322 points) ⇅

🏳 Sakartwelos Pechburtis Pederazis

❋ 1936

👤 Levan Kobiashvili (100)

⚽ Shota Arveladze (26)

👤 Yes

👟 Adidas

📅 **Biggest Win**
Georgia 7–0 Armenia
(30 March 1997)

Biggest Defeat
Denmark 6–1 Georgia
(7 September 2005)

Competitive Records 🏆

World Cup Never qualified

European Championship
Never qualified

Current Results

Football is in a world of its own. Even though all maps show that Georgia is located in Asia, when it comes to football, they are European and therefore members of UEFA. A wise decision? Judging from the stats, probably not. Despite some notable successes, such as a prominent victory against Bulgaria, the overall picture looks rather bleak for the Eurasians.

GERMANY / UEFA

1st (1602 points) ⇅

🏳 Deutscher Fußball-Bund

☀ 1900

....

👤 Lothar Matthäus (150)

....

⚽ Miroslav Klose (71)

....

👤 Yes

....

👕 Adidas

....

🖩 **Biggest Win**
Germany 16–0 Russian Empire
(1 July 1912)

Biggest Defeat
England (Amateur) 9–0 Germany
(13 March 1909)

Competitive Records 🏆

World Cup Appearances 18
Champions 1954, 1974, 1990, 2014
Qualified for 2018*

European Championship
Appearances 12
Champions 1972, 1980, 1996

....

Current Results

📎 It's safe to say that Bavarian football icons such as Beckenbauer, Müller and Schweinsteiger are aware of the significance of the colours in which they have achieved one victory after the other. When Germany staged its first international match in 1908, the Kingdom of Prussia was the leading power in the German empire, which is why their state colours, black and white, were chosen for the national team strip. Those colours have stuck to this day and that's why most other teams quake in fear when they see the world's number one team line up, resplendent in white and black. By the way, when English fans shout 'Save the Nationalelf!', they are urging their government to invest in free healthcare services. They are not cheering on the German team.

GIBRALTAR / UEFA

206th (0 points)

Gibraltar Football Association

1895

Liam Walker (28)

Lee Casciaro (2), Jake Gosling (2)

-

Admiral

Biggest Win
Gibraltar 1–0 Malta
(4 June 2014)

Biggest Defeat
Belgium 9–0 Gibraltar
(31 August 2017)

Competitive Records

World Cup Never qualified

European Championship
Never qualified

Current Results

Clausewitz said that football is an extension of politics by other means. Just because Spain to this day will not accept the 1713 loss of this strategically important territory to the British, it has permanently tried to hold Gibraltar's entry into UEFA back. But, in 2013, they could not prevent this tiny sovereignty becoming a fully-fledged member of UEFA and eventually of FIFA three years later. A success indeed, but not so far on the soccer pitch. Even the mighty Danny Higginbotham, nephew of the then manager, was unable to help them with that.

GREECE / UEFA

47th (680 points)

🏳 Elliniki Podosferiki Omospondia

❄ 1926

👤 Giorgos Karagounis (139)

⚽ Nikolaos Anastopoulos (29)

👤 Yes

👟 Nike

📅 **Biggest Win**
Greece 8–0 Syria
(25 November 1949)

Biggest Defeat
Hungary 11–1 Greece
(25 March 1938)

Competitive Records 🏆

World Cup Appearances 3
Round of 16 2014

European Championship
Appearances 4
Champions 2004

Current Results

For a long time, the most memorable football game involving the Greeks was the 1972 Monty Python sketch featuring philosophers from ancient Greece playing against their counterparts from Germany. However, the two nations did truly join forces and write football history for Greece in 2004. The Greeks became European champions under the guidance of their German coach, Otto Rehhagel.

HUNGARY / UEFA

HUN

53rd (630 points)

Magyar Labdarúgó Szövetség

1901

Gábor Király (108)

Ferenc Puskás (84)

Yes

Adidas

Biggest Win
Russia 0–12 Hungary (14 July 1912); Albania 0–12 Hungary (24 September 1950)

Biggest Defeat
Netherlands 8–1 Hungary (11 October 2013)

Competitive Records

World Cup Appearances 9
Runners-up 1938, 1954

European Championship
Appearances 3
Third place 1964

Current Results

The Magyars are among the veterans of global football. In 1902, they played against Austria in the first international match between two non-British European teams. In the 1950s, Ferenc Puskás' 'Golden Eleven' remained undefeated for 31 games in a row, in the course of which they beat England 6–3. Their breathtaking triumph ended, as so many do, against West Germany in 1954 at the World Cup final in Bern. The golden age of Hungarian dominance came to an end thanks to a shower of rain and Adolf Dassler's latest innovation – the screw-in stud. Well, at least, that's what happened according to Sönke Wortmann's brilliant film *The Miracle of Bern*.

IRELAND / UEFA

32nd (798 points) ⇅

🏳 Football Association of Ireland

❄ 1921

👤 Robbie Keane (146)

🔫 Robbie Keane (68)

👤 Yes

🚌 Umbro

🖩 **Biggest Win**
Ireland 8–0 Malta
(16 November 1983)

Biggest Defeat
Brazil 7–0 Ireland
(27 May 1982)

Competitive Records 🏆

World Cup Appearances 3
Quarter-finals 1990

European Championship
Appearances 3
Rounds of 16 2016

Current Results

📎 English-born World Cup winner Jack Charlton led his Irish team to success in the 80s and 90s with one brilliant idea. He searched abroad for players, who hadn't made the cut in their own national association but, thanks to the great Irish diaspora, could claim Irish citizenship by dint of their ancestry. This ingenious loophole contributed largely to Ireland being able to qualify for their first European Championship in 1988 and the World Cup in 1990. Some quipped that the Football Association of Ireland (FAI) had become an acronym for Find An Irishman and pressure led to them toning down the policy. But, when you listen nowadays to Charlton's former players commentating on the radio, you may be forgiven for being confused by the thick Glaswegian accent of Ray Houghton, the Kentish drawl of Andy Townsend, the cockney lilt of Matt Holland and the Scouse-inflected Welsh of Kevin Sheedy – all Irish, to a man.

ICELAND / UEFA

22nd (910 points) ⇅

🏴 Knattspyrnusamband Íslands

❋ 1947

👤 Rúnar Kristinsson (104)

🔫 Eiður Guðjohnsen (26)

👤 Yes

🚌 Erreà

📅 **Biggest Win**
Iceland 5–0 Malta
(27 July 2000)

Biggest Defeat
Denmark 14–2 Iceland
(23 August 1967)

Competitive Records 🏆

World Cup
Qualified for 2018* (first time)

European Championship
Appearances 1 (2016)
Quarter-finals 2016

Current Results

📎 The so called 'Huh' Viking war chant of the Icelandic fans is enough to make any team shudder. Surprisingly, they knocked England out in the quarter-finals of the European Championship in 2016 and their qualification for the 2018 World Cup was sensational. Given they are by far the smallest country ever to reach the finals of this big tournament – 'Huh' indeed!

* Kit as far as known 3 January 2018

ISRAEL / UEFA

98th (355 points) ⇅

🏳 Israel Football Association

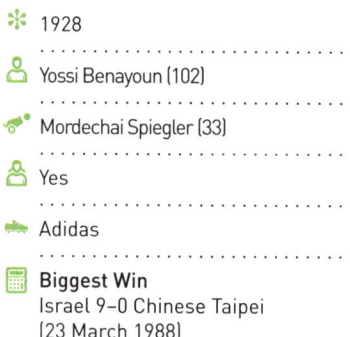

✳ 1928
....

👤 Yossi Benayoun (102)
....

⚽ Mordechai Spiegler (33)
....

👤 Yes
....

👕 Adidas
....

📅 **Biggest Win**
Israel 9–0 Chinese Taipei
(23 March 1988)

Biggest Defeat
Germany 7–1 Israel
(13 February 2002)

Competitive Records 🏆

World Cup Appearances 1
Group stage 1970

European Championship
Never qualified

Asian Cup Appearances 4
Champions 1964
....

Current Results

📎 The team has been in exile for over 40 years. A boycott by the Arab states expelled Israel from the Asian Association in 1974 and they were forced to compete in the Oceania World Cup qualifier group in 1985. Following the dissolution of the Eastern Bloc, however, which had hitherto blocked their admission, Israel finally became a member of UEFA in 1991.

ITALY / UEFA

14th (1052 points) ⇅

🏳 **Federazione Italiana Giuoco Calcio**

✳ 1898

👤 Gianluigi Buffon (173)

🔫 Luigi Riva (35)

👤 Yes

👟 Puma

🧮 **Biggest Win**
Italy 9–0 USA
(2 August 1948)

Biggest Defeat
Hungary 7–1 Italy
(6 April 1924)

Competitive Records 🏆

World Cup Appearances 18
Champions 1934, 1938, 1982, 2006

European Championship
Appearances 9
Champions 1968

Current Results

✏

With four world titles under their belts, the Azzurri number among the best teams in the world. Out of the countless big matches they have played down the years, there is one that stands out in particular. The Game of the Century took place against West Germany in the semi-finals of the World Cup in Mexico in 1970. Italy beat the ten and a half men of West Germany by 4–3 after extra time in the Aztec Stadium. Franz 'der Kaiser' Beckenbauer had been playing with his arm in a sling for the best part of an hour after dislocating his shoulder in a crunching tackle. This epic battle is commemorated by a plaque outside the stadium thanking both teams for the enduring spirit and sporting bravery.

KAZAKHSTAN / UEFA

136th (220 points)

Qasaqstannyng Futbol Federazijassy

1914

Samat Smakov (76)

Ruslan Baltiev (13)

Yes

Adidas

Biggest Win
Pakistan 0–7 Kazakhstan
(11 June 1997)

Biggest Defeat
Kazakhstan 0–6 Turkey (8 June 2005);
Russia 6–0 Kazakhstan (23 May 2008)

Competitive Records

World Cup Never qualified

European Championship
Never qualified

Asian Cup Never qualified

Current Results

There is something reminiscent of Josef Stalin in the Kazakh coach's team selection. The former Soviet leader banished many native Russian Germans to Kazakhstan in the aftermath of Germany's invasion in 1941. Six of their descendants have already represented Kazakhstan on the international stage, but they have been beaten four times against the land of their forefathers.

KOSOVO / UEFA

174th (97 points)

🏳 Federata e Futbollit e Kosovës

2000

Samir Ujkani (15)

Albert Bunjaku (3)

Yes

Kelme

Biggest Win
Kosovo 2–0 Faroe Islands
(3 June 2016)

Biggest Defeat
Kosovo 0–6 Croatia
(6 October 2016)

Competitive Records

World Cup Never qualified

European Championship
Never qualified

Current Results

The name Kosovo actually means 'blackbird field'. Historically, Kosovo has been the scene of battles and conflicts, from the clashes between Christians and Ottomans to the more recent Kosovo conflict in 1999. The latter is responsible for there being barely anything to report about. In all fairness to Kosovo, its national team has only been competing on an international level since 2016.

1

2

LIECHTENSTEIN / UEFA

187th (54 points)

🏳 Liechtensteiner Fussballverband

※ 1934

👤 Mario Frick (130)

🔫 Mario Frick (16)

👤 -

🚗 Adidas

🖩 **Biggest Win**
Luxembourg 0–4 Liechtenstein
(13 October 2004)

Biggest Defeat
Liechtenstein 1–11 Macedonia
(9 November 1996)

Competitive Records 🏆

World Cup Never qualified

European Championship
Never qualified

Current Results

📎 **Many still regard the principality as a tax haven. Football is not the first thing that springs to mind when thinking about Liechtenstein and its 37,500 inhabitants. If you exclude women, children and old people, the national team almost picks itself. This, therefore, puts their victories against larger nations such as Azerbaijan and Latvia into an even more glowing perspective.**

LITHUANIA / UEFA

148th (179 points)

🚩 Lietuvos futbolo federacija

✳ 1922

👤 Andrius Skerla (84)

🔫 Tomas Danilevičius (19)

👤 Yes

👕 Hummel

🧮 **Biggest Win**
Lithuania 7–0 Estonia
(20 May 1995)

Biggest Defeat
Lithuania 0–10 Egypt
(1 June 1924)

Competitive Records 🏆

World Cup Never qualified

European Championship
Never qualified

Current Results

📎 **Basketball is the big thing in Lithuania with its basketball team one of the best in Europe. That does not stop the less respected national football team from making life difficult for the bigger players. They defied the odds with draws against multiple world champions Italy and Germany. Not only that, but these matches were played in the away stadia.**

LUXEMBOURG / UEFA

84th (407 points) ⇅

🏳 Fédération Luxembourgeoise de Football

✳ 1908

👤 Jeff Strasser (98)

⚽ Léon Mart (16)

👤 Yes

👟 Adidas

🖩 **Biggest Win**
Luxembourg 6–0 Afghanistan
(26 July 1948)

Biggest Defeat
Luxembourg 0–9 England (19 October
1960); England 9–0 Luxembourg
(15 December 1982)

Competitive Records 🏆

World Cup Never qualified

European Championship
Never qualified

Current Results

📎 **Football fans have to be schooled with a certain ability to suffer, especially for those who are fans of the underdog. The agony that Luxembourg fans had to endure between 1980 and 1985 is, however, heart-wrenching. Their team were defeated an incredible 35 times in a row.**

LATVIA / UEFA

131st (233 points) ⇅

⚑ Latvijas Futbola federācija

✳ 1921

👤 Vitalijs Astafjevs (167)

⚽ Maris Verpakovskis (29)

👤 Yes

👕 Adidas

📅 **Biggest Win**
Estonia 1–8 Latvia
(18 August 1942)

Biggest Defeat
Sweden 12–0 Latvia
(29 May 1927)

Competitive Records 🏆

World Cup Never qualified

European Championship
Appearances 1
Group stage 2004

Current Results

📎 Football is no longer a side-show to ice hockey or basketball in Latvia and that is probably down to the team's performances at the Euros in 2004. They defied the odds in the group stage by securing a draw against favourites Germany. Without having ever played in a World Cup, Vitalijs Astafjevs is one of the world's record-breaking internationals with 167 caps.

MOLDOVA / UEFA

166th (111 points) ↕

🏳 Federaţia Moldovenească de Fotbal

✳ 1990

....

👤 Alexandru Epureanu (76/83)

....

⚽ Serghei Cleşcenco (11)

....

👤 Yes

....

👟 Jako

....

🖩 **Biggest Win**
Moldova 5–0 Pakistan
(18 August 1992)

Biggest Defeat
Sweden 6–0 Moldova
(6 June 2001)

Competitive Records 🏆

World Cup Never qualified

European Championship
Never qualified

....

Current Results

📎 There is no doubt that anyone can finish in last place. Yet to finish behind a small state like Liechtenstein is what the majority of fans would
call ignominy. Moldova played twice against the tiny principality in the
2016 European Championship qualifiers, but only managed to score
one point. The other point, gained in the draw against Russia, was a
mere consolation.

MACEDONIA / UEFA

76th (446 points) ↕

🏳 **Fudbalska Federacija na Makedonija**

✳ 1926
....

👤 Goce Sedloski (100)
....

🎯 Goran Pandev (30)
....

👤 Yes
....

👕 Jako
....

🖩 **Biggest Win**
Liechtenstein 1–11 Macedonia
(9 November 1996)

Biggest Defeat
Hungary 5–0 Macedonia (14 November 2001); Czech Republic 6–1
Macedonia (8 June 2005)

Competitive Records 🏆

World Cup Never qualified

European Championship
Never qualified
....

Current Results

📎 **Macedonia's national team seem to be suffering from some type of 'Robin Hood' syndrome. In the qualifying matches for international tournaments, they seem to take points from the big teams and give them away to the lowly ones. For example, draws against teams such as England, Holland and Turkey have been pulled off, yet the team has been beaten by Azerbaijan, Liechtenstein and Andorra.**

1

2

MALTA / UEFA

181st (66 points) ⇅

🏳 Malta Football Association

❄ 1900

👤 Michael Mifsud (125)

🏹 Michael Mifsud (40)

👤 Yes

👕 Givova

🖩 **Biggest Win**
Malta 7–1 Liechtenstein
(26 March 2008)

Biggest Defeat
Spain 12–1 Malta
(21 December 1983)

Competitive Records 🏆

World Cup Never qualified

European Championship
Never qualified

Current Results

📎 **Most opposing fans typically see Malta as an easy target and the Maltese confirmed this in 1984 with a rotten performance against Spain. The Iberians needed to score by a margin of 11 goals to qualify for the European Championship. They ended up beating Malta 12–1 and the match triggered much talk of match fixing. Let it not be forgotten, however, that Malta can actually win games, too. In the past, they have enjoyed wins over teams such as Greece and Hungary.**

MONTENEGRO / UEFA

46th (681 points)

Fudbalski savez Crne Gore

❄ 1931

👤 Elsad Zverotić (61)

🔫 Stevan Jovetic (24)

👤 Yes

🚗 Legea

🧮 **Biggest Win**
San Marino 0–6 Montenegro
(11 September 2012)

Biggest Defeat
Romania 4–0 Montenegro (31 May
2008); Montenegro 0–4 Ukraine
(7 June 2013)

Competitive Records

World Cup
Group stage 2006

European Championship
Never qualified

Current Results

📎 They say that the roar of the fans can act as a twelfth man, but sometimes their antics can also achieve the opposite. In 2015, Montenegro held Russia at 0–0 up to the 67th minute. The Russian goalkeeper was hit by a firecracker, and further objects continued to fly on to the pitch so that the match had to be abandoned and a 3–0 win was awarded to Russia.

NETHERLANDS / UEFA

KNVB

20th (952 points) ↕

🏳 Koninklijke Nederlandse Voetbal Bond

❄ 1889

👤 Wesley Sneijder (132)

⚽ Robin van Persie (50)

👤 Yes

🚚 Nike

📅 **Biggest Win**
Netherlands 11–0 San Marino
(2 September 2011)

Biggest Defeat
Netherlands 2–12 England
(1 April 1907)

Competitive Records 🏆

World Cup Appearances 10
Runners-up 1974, 1978, 2010

European Championship
Appearances 9
Champions 1988

Current Results

📎 Fighting against the Spanish Empire back in the 17th century, the Dutch would sing the patriotic song 'Oranje Boven', the words of which translate roughly as 'Hold your orange banners aloft, lads! Long live the queen!' In later years, when it came to football, these skillful players decked out in bright orange became a world power themselves. Three times World Cup runners-up, the Netherlands have produced genius after genius. Johan Cruyff, in particular, was one of the all-time greatest. Like Garrincha, Maradona, Zidane and David Rocastle, Cruyff is one of the few footballers to have a move named after him. Cruyff embodied the concept of Total Football and developed the system into the coolest tactical theory in the modern game.

NORTHERN IRELAND / UEFA

24th (867 points) ⇅

🏴 Irish Football Association

✳ 1880

👤 Pat Jennings (119)

⚽ David Healy (36)

👤 Yes

🚗 Adidas

🖩 **Biggest Win**
Ireland 7–0 Wales
(1 February 1930)

Biggest Defeat
Ireland 0–13 England
(18 February 1882)

Competitive Records 🏆

World Cup Appearances 3
Quarter-finals 1958

European Championship
Appearances 1
Round of 16 2016

Current Results

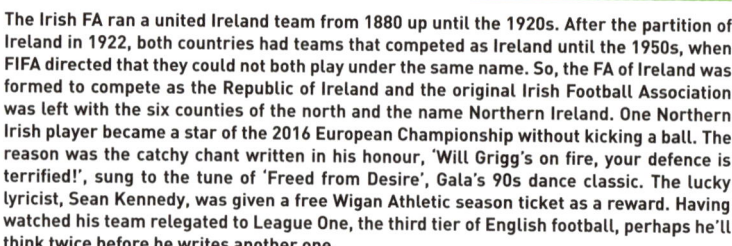

The Irish FA ran a united Ireland team from 1880 up until the 1920s. After the partition of Ireland in 1922, both countries had teams that competed as Ireland until the 1950s, when FIFA directed that they could not both play under the same name. So, the FA of Ireland was formed to compete as the Republic of Ireland and the original Irish Football Association was left with the six counties of the north and the name Northern Ireland. One Northern Irish player became a star of the 2016 European Championship without kicking a ball. The reason was the catchy chant written in his honour, 'Will Grigg's on fire, your defence is terrified!', sung to the tune of 'Freed from Desire', Gala's 90s dance classic. The lucky lyricist, Sean Kennedy, was given a free Wigan Athletic season ticket as a reward. Having watched his team relegated to League One, the third tier of English football, perhaps he'll think twice before he writes another one.

NORWAY / UEFA

58th (573 points)

⚑ Norges Fotballforbund

❄ 1902

....

👤 John Arne Riise (110)

....

⚽ Jørgen Juve (33)

....

👤 Yes

....

👟 Nike

....

🖩 **Biggest Win**
Norway 12–0 Finland
(28 June 1946)

Biggest Defeat
Denmark 12–0 Norway
(7 October 1917)

🏆 **Competitive Records**

World Cup Appearances 3
Rounds of 16 1998

European Championship
Appearances 1
Group stage 2000

....

Current Results

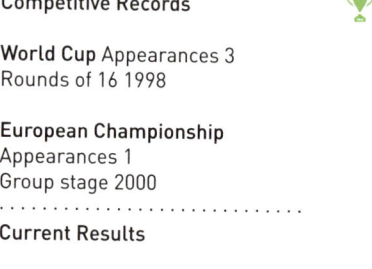

📎 What country in the world can claim to have an unbeaten international record against the mighty Brazil? Little Norway, of course! With two draws and two wins, their claim is pretty impressive. However, since there are a number of other countries out there who they generally fare less well against, Norway's tournament successes are a distance away. Many may remember Bjørge Lillelien's hilarious outburst after his national team beat England 2–1 in a World Cup qualifier in Oslo in 1981. After reeling off a long list of English luminaries from Lord Nelson to Maggie Thatcher, the excited commentator declared, 'Your boys took one hell of a beating!'

POLAND / UEFA

7th (1209 points) ⇅

🏳 Polski Związek Piłki Nożnej

✳ 1919

👤 Michał Żewłakow (102)

🔫 Robert Lewandowski (51)

👤 Yes

👟 Nike

 **Biggest Win**
Poland 10–0 San Marino
(1 April 2009)

Biggest Defeat
Denmark 8–0 Poland (26 June 1948)

Competitive Records 🏆

World Cup Appearances 7
Third place 1974, 1982
Qualified for 2018*

European Championship
Appearances 3
Quarter-finals 2016

Current Results ✏

📎 Perhaps even more notoriously than ensuring England didn't travel to West Germany in 1974 after goalie Jan Tomasewski, who Brian Clough had earlier dubbed a 'clown', saved a penalty, the Polish national team were involved in the one of the best games in World Cup history, when they made their first appearance in France in 1938. It was not until late in extra time that they went down to Brazil by six goals to five. Ernst Willimowski was the first player at a finals event to hit four goals in one game. There would be other big showdowns to come and Poland's best return in world soccer so far has been third place twice.

* Kit as far as known 3 January 2018

PORTUGAL / UEFA

3rd (1358 points)

🏴 Federação Portuguesa de Futebol

✳ 1914

👤 Cristiano Ronaldo (147)

⚽ Cristiano Ronaldo (79)

👤 Yes

👟 Nike

📅 **Biggest Win**
Portugal 8–0 Liechtenstein (9 June 1999); Portugal 8–0 Kuwait (19 November 2003)

Biggest Defeat
Portugal 0–10 England (25 May 1947)

Competitive Records 🏆

World Cup Appearances 7
Third place 1966
Qualified for 2018*

European Championship
Appearances 7
Champions 2016

Current Results

📎 **There was nothing that Cristiano Ronaldo wanted more than to win a title with Portugal. And then something bizarre happened. In the final of the 2016 European Championship, Ronaldo was injured and stretchered off in tears in the 25th minute. Everyone thought that, without their golden boy, his team had no chance against the heavily fancied French, but the Team of the Five Forts nevertheless won the match 1–0. All of Portugal cheered, as did Cristiano, albeit not quite as vehemently as if he'd stayed on the pitch.**

* Kit as far as known 3 January 2018

ROMANIA / UEFA

41st (737 points)

Federaţia Română de Fotbal

1909

Dorinel Munteanu (134)

Gheorghe Hagi (35), Adrian Mutu (35)

Yes

Joma

Biggest Win
Romania 9–0 Finland
(14 October 1973)

Biggest Defeat
Hungary 9–0 Romania
(6 June 1948)

Competitive Records

World Cup Appearances 7
Quarter-finals 1994

European Championship
Appearances 5
Quarter-finals 2000

Current Results

The fall of communism also saw the rise to the big time for the Romanian national football team. The highlight was the World Cup finals in the USA in 1994. In the knock-out stages, their Gheorghe 'Regele' (The King) Hagi inspired team overcame the runners-up from the previous World Cup – they beat Argentina 3–2. The match was widely chosen as the game of the tournament. The Romanians finally went down in a penalty shoot-out to Sweden in the quarter-final but Hagi, Popescu, Dumitrescu, Raducioiu and Petrescu had already signed their names into the World Cup history book.

RUSSIA / UEFA

65th (534 points)

⚐ Rossijski Futbolny Sojus

❋ 1931

. . . .

👤 Sergei Ignashevich (120)

. . . .

Aleksandr Kerzhakov (30)

. . . .

👤 Yes

. . . .

🚌 Adidas

. . . .

📅 **Biggest Win**
San Marino 0–7 Russia (7 June 1995);
Liechtenstein 0–7 Russia (8 September 2015)

Biggest Defeat
Germany 16–0 Russia
(1 July 1912)

Competitive Records 🏆

World Cup Appearances 11
Fourth place 1966
Qualified for 2018*

European Championship
Appearances 10
Champions 1960

. . . .

Current Results

📎 The USSR produced the greatest goalkeeper in the history of the game – Lev Yashin, known as The Black Spider, because of his predilection for an all-black kit. With Yashin in the nets, the Soviet Union finished fourth at the World Cup in England in 1966. After the breakup of the Soviet Union, the team's official name became the CIS national team, which wasn't particularly snappy. Eventually, they became simply Russia in 1992. The disintegration of the vast Soviet empire led to much bloodletting in the sense that the pool of players from which they could select decreased dramatically. The Baltic and central Asian states formed their own national teams and the Ukrainian stars, who had been the backbone of the successful side that, under manager Guus Hiddink, finished runners-up to Holland in Euro 1988, were no longer available. This does not bode well for when they host the World Cup in 2018.

SCOTLAND / UEFA

32nd (798 points) ↕

⚑ Scottish Football Association

✳ 1873

. . . .

👤 Kenny Dalglish (102)

. . . .

⚽ Kenny Dalglish (30), Denis Law (30)

. . . .

👕 Yes

. . . .

👟 Adidas

. . . .

🖩 **Biggest Win**
Scotland 11–0 Ireland
(23 February 1901)

Biggest Defeat
Uruguay 7–0 Scotland
(19 June 1954)

Competitive Records 🏆

World Cup Appearances 8
First group stage 1974

European Championship
Appearances 2
Last 8 1992

. . . .

Current Results

✎

📎 **If you spot the ref wearing red, then it might be down to the Scots. Their dark blue shirts are easily mistaken for black. Along with England, Scotland are the auldest team in the world and they have punched above their weight over the last 150 years considering the population is only a tenth of England's. They have made it to the World Cup finals eight times but were eliminated at the group stage on each occasion. Their most unfortunate exit from the tournament, in 1974, when they had to say goodbye despite not losing a single game, is still bemoaned over a pint of heavy in pubs from Dumfries to Inverness every night.**

SAN MARINO / UEFA

204th (11 points)

Federazione Sammarinese Giuoco Calcio

1931

Andy Selva (74)

Andy Selva (8)

-

Adidas

Biggest Win
San Marino 1–0 Liechtenstein
(28 April 2004)

Biggest Defeat
San Marino 0–13 Germany
(6 September 2006)

Competitive Records

World Cup Never qualified

European Championship
Never qualified

Current Results

Not all national team players are overpaid professionals, certainly not those of San Marino. Some work in factories or earn their money selling computers or jeans. The stats speak for themselves. So far, they have only managed to win one match, beating Liechtenstein 1–0. Their other matches have resulted in four draws and 139 defeats with a current goal difference of 22–624. Ouch!

SERBIA / UEFA

37th (756 points)

⚑ Fudbalski savez Srbije

✳ 1919

👤 Branislav Ivanović (81)

⚽ Nikola Žigić (16)

👤 Yes

👕 Umbro

🧮 **Biggest Win**
Serbia 5–0 Romania (10 October 2009); Serbia 6–1 Wales (11 September 2012)

Biggest Defeat
Serbia 0–3 Belgium
(12 October 2012)

Competitive Records 🏆

World Cup Appearances
Group stage 2006 (as Serbia-Montenegro), 2010
Qualified for 2018*

European Championship
Never qualified

Current Results

📎 **Not only must a Serbian international player be a good footballer, he also has to be a good singer. In 2012, Adem Ljajić did not join in the singing of the national anthem and was promptly kicked off the team. They did not have much success in that European Championship anyway, but they were all on the same hymn sheet when they reached the group stages in the 2010 World Cup in South Africa, which remains their biggest achievement to date.**

* Kit as far as known 3 January 2018

SWITZERLAND / UEFA

8th (1190 points)

🏳 Schweizerischer Fussballverband

✳ 1895

👤 Heinz Hermann (118)

⚽ Alex Frei (42)

👤 Yes

👟 Nike

🧮 **Biggest Win**
Switzerland 9–0 Lithuania
(25 May 1924)

Biggest Defeat
Hungary 9–0 Switzerland
(29 October 1911)

Competitive Records 🏆

World Cup Appearances 10
Quarter-finals 1934, 1938, 1954
Qualified for 2018*

European Championship
Appearances 4
Round of 16 2016

Current Results

📎 **The European Championship qualifier against France in 2016 was a disaster. Not for the Swiss team, as such, but for the manufacturer of their shirts. Seven of the shirts had to be shredded. The reason being, according to the manufacturer, that they were made from a batch of faulty materials. One Swiss player quipped that he hoped the manufacturer would not start producing contraceptives.**

* Kit as far as known 3 January 2018

SLOVAKIA / UEFA

28th (817 points)

Slovenský futbalový zväz

1938

Miroslav Karhan (107)

Róbert Vittek (23)

Yes

Nike

Biggest Win
Slovakia 7–0 San Marino (13 October 2007); Slovakia 7–0 San Marino (6 June 2009)

Biggest Defeat
Argentina 6–0 Slovakia
(22 June 1995)

Competitive Records

World Cup Appearances 1
Round of 16 2010

European Championship
Appearances 1
Round of 16 201

Current Results

Before the team began their renaissance, they had to come to terms with their separation from the Czech Republic in 1993. Slovak players had enjoyed considerable success with the combined Czechoslovakia national team between 1930 and 1994, but had to start all over again after independence. Slovakia have since proved that they can hold their own with the big boys. They reached the knock-out stages at the 2010 World Cup and managed to do so again at the Euros in France 2016.

SLOVENIA / UEFA

NZS

69th (522 points)

⇅

🏳 **Nogometna zveza Slovenije**

✳ 1920

👤 Boštjan Cesar (100)

🔫 Zlatko Zahovič (35)

👤 Yes

👟 Nike

📋 **Biggest Win**
Oman 0–7 Slovenia
(8 February 1999)

Biggest Defeat
France 5–0 Slovenia
(12 October 2002)

Competitive Records 🏆

World Cup Appearances 2
Group stage 2002, 2010

European Championship
Appearances 1
Group stage 2000

Current Results

📎 Given that the entire country has fewer inhabitants than some major European cities and also that the team has only existed since 1991, Slovenia's achievements are quite impressive. The Slovenians have qualified twice for the World Cup finals and once for the European Championship, too. The best Slovenian player, Branko Oblak, once played for the 'old' Yugoslavia.

SWEDEN / UEFA

18th (998 points)

🚩 Svenska Fotbollförbundet

✳ 1904

👤 Anders Svensson (148)

⚽ Zlatan Ibrahimović (62)

👤 Yes

👕 Adidas

🗒 **Biggest Win**
Sweden 12–0 Latvia (29 August 1927);
Sweden 12–0 South Korea (5 August 1948)

Biggest Defeat
Great Britain 12–1 Sweden
(20 October 1908)

🏆 **Competitive Records**

World Cup Appearances 12
Runners-up 1958
Qualified for 2018*

European Championship
Appearances 6
Semi-finals 1992

Current Results

📎 The Swedish national team were the first to play over a thousand international games. This is not down to their having started playing games sooner than everybody else, but because the pacifist nation was able to avoid major wars, enabling its team to play football while other countries fought each other. In 1958, with home advantage, the Swedes were World Cup runners-up, and they won gold at the 1948 Olympics in London ten years earlier.

TURKEY / UEFA

42nd (735 points) ↕

🏳 **Türkiye Futbol Federasyonu**

❋ 1923

👤 Rüştü Reçber (120)

🔫 Hakan Şükür (51)

👤 Yes

👕 Nike

🧮 **Biggest Win**
Turkey 7–0 San Marino
(10 November 1996)

Biggest Defeat
England 8–0 Turkey
(14 October 1987)

🏆 **Competitive Records**

World Cup Appearances 2
Third place 2002

European Championship
Appearances 4
Semi-finals 2008

Current Results

📎 **The new millennium could not have started any better for the boys from the Bosphorus. The team took third place at the World Cup finals in Japan and South Korea in 2002, reached the semis of the 2008 European Championship and moved into the world's top ten international rankings. In the meantime, however, things are not looking so rosy for the Crescent Stars. The star player of their best ever team, Hakan Şükür, is wanted for arrest as a sympathiser of the Gülen religious movement. But the Turks continue to unearth fresh talent and Danish-born Emre Mor is expected to shine in future.**

UKRAINE / UEFA

UKRAINE

35th (781 points) ⇅

🏳 Federaziya Futbolu Ukrayiny

❄ 1991

👤 Anatoliy Tymoshchuk (144)

⚽ Andriy Shevchenko (48)

👤 Yes

👟 Joma

🖩 **Biggest Win**
Ukraine 9–0 San Marino
(6 September 2013)

Biggest Defeat
Spain 4–0 Ukraine (14 June 2006);
Czech Republic 4–0 Ukraine
(6 September 2011)

Competitive Records 🏆

World Cup Appearances 1
Quarter-finals 2006

European Championship
Appearances 2
Group stage 2012, 2016

Current Results

✏

📎 **Before losing the Crimea, Ukraine had already lost a few important players to Russia, whose citizenships were accepted after the collapse of the Soviet Union. One of those players was Oleg Salenko, top goal scorer at the 1994 World Cup in the USA. In spite of this, the Ukrainian national team reached the quarter-finals of the 2006 World Cup in Germany, which is more than can be said for the Russians.**

WALES / UEFA

19th (985 points) ↑↓

🏳 Football Association of Wales

※ 1876

👤 Neville Southall (92)

🔫 Ian Rush (28)

👤 Yes

🚗 Adidas

🗓 **Biggest Win**
Wales 11–0 Ireland
(3 March 1888)

Biggest Defeat
Scotland 9–0 Wales
(23 March 1878)

Competitive Records 🏆

World Cup Appearances 1
Quarter-finals 1958

European Championship
Appearances 1
Semi-finals 2016

Current Results

📎 The FIFA World Ranking of September 2016 is likely to have been print-ed out and admired by Welshfolk from the Brecon Beacons to Blaenau Ffestiniog. The team was ranked ninth in the world, one place ahead of England – the motherland of football. In 2016, the team reached the semi-finals of the European Championship and were only narrowly defeated by eventual champions Portugal. But their 2018 World Cup hopes were dashed by fellow Celts Republic of Ireland with a 1–0 loss in Cardiff in October 2017.

Team's Acknowledgements

The world is awash with football experts, each of them rich in sundry football information, facts and visual recollections, not to forget the insights of the individual players themselves and their own input.

We would like to thank everyone who helped us with guidance and resources, as well as all those we were unable to catch up with. One thing made clear to us while putting this project together was simple: even with football facts, there will constantly be an array of 'informers'. Yet, regardless of the endless supply of information on whatever subject matter, how to use the data available is something that needs to be decided on.

First and foremost we thank Ursula Steffens, who had the idea for this book. Further thanks goes to: Tobias Anding, Matthias Bolhöfer, Andrew Hansen, Christian Rieker, Nicolas Roos, Andreas Karl Schulze, Jill von Velsen, Friedrich Zimmermann.

© Prestel Verlag, Munich · London · New York, 2018
A member of Verlagsgruppe Random House GmbH
Neumarkter Strasse 28 · 81673 München

www.prestel.de

Texts: Michael Brepohl
Illustrations: Paul and Dirk Uhlenbrock
Translation: Paul Kelly
Text Editor: Andrew Hansen
Editorial Management: Nicola von Velsen
Research: Michael Brepohl, Andrew Hansen, Melanie Kattanek, Dirk Uhlenbrock,
Paul Uhlenbrock, Nicola von Velsen
Copy Editing: Graham Hughes

Layout: Dirk Uhlenbrock
Production Management: Friederike Schirge
Reprographics: Reproline Mediateam
Printing and Binding: TBB a.s. Banská Bystrica
Paper: Tauro Offset
Fonts: Goal, FF Din

Verlagsgruppe Random House FSC

Printed in Slovakia
ISBN 978-3-7913-8439-9